Langenscheidt

German Grammar
in a Nutshell

Deutsche Grammatik — kurz und schmerzlos

Von Christine Stief und Christian Stang

Langenscheidt

München · Wien

Herausgegeben von der Langenscheidt-Redaktion
Neu bearbeitet von Georgette Liedtke
Illustrationen: Claas Janssen, www.janssen-illustration.de
Projektmanagement: Anne Ley-Schalles
Layout: Ute Weber
Umschlaggestaltung: KW 43 BRANDDESIGN

Laden Sie sich auf www.langenscheidt.de/kurzundschmerzlos mit dem Code kus887 kostenlos zusätzliche Übungen herunter.

Die Symbole:

🛈 Spezielle Spracheigenheit des Deutschen

☼ Merksatz

⚡ Vorsicht, Stolperstein!

◖ Ausnahme oder Sonderform

➡ Unterschiede zum Deutschen

L! Lerntipp

➕ Hilfestellung

▷ Verweis auf zusammenhängende
Grammatikthemen

© 2013 by Langenscheidt KG, Berlin und München

Satz: Franzis print & media GmbH, München
Druck und Bindung: Stürtz GmbH, Würzburg

ISBN 978-3-468-34887-7

13011

Contents

Contents

Contents

Contents

Vorwort   Preface

Maybe you've considered German grammar to be difficult – until now. This short and entertaining little book will show you that this is not quite so and that German grammar can be quite fun! It has been specially designed to help non-native speakers of German to master the basic rules of the language – as briefly and painlessly as possible. It makes no pretence at being *exhaustive*.

The grammar content of this book is based on general everyday usage in the German-speaking countries of Germany, Austria and Switzerland. All the headings, explanations, tips and reminders are in English. To make things even easier we have also translated the German examples illustrating the rules into English. The numbering system makes it easy to find your way and to repeat or revise material in any order.

An important new feature in this grammar book is its communicative approach. It's not the bare rules of grammar that take prominence but the way elements of language function as a means of communication. "What is my partner saying to me and how is he/she saying it?"

German Grammar in a Nutshell is practical, easy to understand and amusing, so you should have no great difficulty in "cracking" it! The motto being: the more unusual the situation, the better you remember the rule.

And one last tip: Don't try to devour the whole book at once! Despite its light and airy presentation it might prove to be too much to digest and spoil your appetite. Much better to enjoy the menu in small manageable portions and still have room for more!

The authors and publishers wish you every success with this book and hope you enjoy using it.

1 Artikel Articles
oder *Der Mann, das Kind, die Frau*

Der Geiger spielt. Die Sängerin singt. Das Handy klingelt.

The violonist is playing. The singer is singing. The mobile phone is ringing.

In German, as in English, nouns are not normally used on their own. They are almost always preceded by an article:

der Koffer, **der** Computer	*the suitcase, the computer*
das Fahrrad, **das** Handy	*the bike, the mobile phone*
die Tasche, **die** Zeitung	*the bag, the newspaper*

In German the definite article tells us three things about the noun depending on how it is used in the sentence:
- the gender: either *masculine* der, *neuter* das or *feminine* die
- the number: *singular* or *plural*
  and also something typical for the German language:
- the case: *nominative* (nom.), *accusative* (acc.), *dative* (dat.) or *genitive* (gen.)

Das ist **der** Koffer. *That's the suitcase.*
(masculine, singular, nom.)
Ich trage **den** Koffer. *I'll carry the suitcase.*
(masculine, singular, acc.)
Er kommt mit **dem** Zug. *He's coming by train.*
(masculine, singular, dat.)

In German, as in English, there are different kinds of
articles, as you'll see on the following pages.

1.1 Unbestimmte und bestimmte Artikel
Indefinite and Definite Articles
oder *Ein Mann – der Mann, eine Frau –
die Frau*

Gleich kommt eine
Frau und sagt, dass sie
ein Kind verloren hat.
Sagen Sie der Frau, dass
das Kind in der
Spielwarenabteilung
ist.

A woman will turn up in a moment. She'll tell you she's lost a child. Tell the woman the child is in the toys department.

When do we use the indefinite and definite articles?

- The indefinite article ein, eine is used just like the English *a/an* if there is only one object or person or if something is new, unknown or non-specific.
- The definite article der, die, das normally refers just like the English *the* to something particular or something we already know.

Es war einmal **ein** König. Der König hatte **eine** Tochter. **Die** Tochter hatte **ein** Pferd …
Once upon a time there was a king. The king had a daughter. The daughter had a horse.
Im Büro: „Ich brauche **einen** Taschenrechner." –
„Nimm doch **den** Rechner im Computer."
In the office: "I need a pocket calculator." – "Use the calculator in the computer."

The negative form of the indefinite article ein, eine is kein, keine:

Hast du **einen** Regenschirm? *Have you got an umbrella?*
Nein, ich habe **keinen** Regenschirm. *No, I haven't got an umbrella.*

The negative of the definite article is formed with nicht, which is placed before the article:

Hier kommt **der** Bus. *Here comes the bus.*
Das ist **nicht der** Bus ins Stadtzentrum. *That's not the bus to the town centre.*

1.2 Artikelformen Forms of the Article
oder *Der Mann, den Mann …*

In German articles change their form depending on how
the nouns they belong to are used in the sentence. They
indicate, as we mentioned above, gender, number and
case. The different forms look like this:

	singular			plural
	masculine	neuter	feminine	
	the man	the child	the woman	people
nom.	der Mann	das Kind	die Frau	die Menschen
	ein	ein	eine	(–)
	kein	kein	keine	keine
acc.	den	das	die	die
	einen	ein	eine	(–)
	keinen	kein	keine	keine
dat.	dem	dem	der	den
	einem	einem	einer	(–)
	keinem	keinem	keiner	keinen
gen.	des	des	der	der
	eines	eines	einer	(–)
	keines	keines	keiner	keiner

The good news is that all these endings are more or less
the same for nouns, pronouns and adjectives. They can
be reduced to a fairly simple table of key signals.

☀ Remember the following key signals:

	masculine	neuter	feminine	plural
nom.	r	s	e	e
acc.	n	s	e	e
dat.	m	m	r	n
gen.	s	s	r	r

☀ There is no indefinite article in the plural:

Diana braucht **einen** Regenschirm. *Diana needs an umbrella.*
Tony verkauft Regenschirme. *Tony sells umbrellas.*

➕ Here are some more points to remember that will help you:
• The plural form is always the same for all genders.
• All the endings for nominative and accusative are the same, except for the masculine singular.
• The endings for masculine <u>und</u> neuter are very often the same.
• The endings for feminine <u>und</u> plural are always the same, except for the dative.

ⓘ In lots of expressions the article is combined with a preposition:

| am (an + dem) | **Am** Freitag kommt der neue Kollege. *Our new colleague arrives on Friday.* |
| ans (an + das) | Frau Mathieu heftet den Zettel **ans** Schwarze Brett. *Frau Mathieu pins the note to the notice-board.* |

aufs (auf + das)	Wir warten **aufs** Frühstück.
	We're waiting for breakfast.
beim (bei + dem)	Herr Peters raucht oft **beim** Telefonieren.
	Herr Peters often smokes while telephoning.
im (in + dem)	Die Präsentation machen wir **im** Hotel „Vier Jahreszeiten".
	We're doing the presentation in the "Four Seasons" Hotel.
ins (in + das)	Heute gehen wir **ins** Kino.
	Today we're going to the cinema.
vom (von + dem)	Herr Runge kommt direkt **vom** Flughafen zu uns.
	Herr Runge is coming here straight from the airport.
zum (zu + dem)	Herr Miller fährt mit dem Taxi **zum** Flughafen.
	Herr Miller is taking a taxi to the airport.
zur (zu + der)	Frau Dupont fährt mit dem Fahrrad **zur** Arbeit.
	Frau Dupont goes to work by bike.

And just one more piece of information to end with: the words dieser, jeder, jener, mancher, solcher, welcher are all declined in the same way as the definite article der.

1.3 Nullartikel **Zero Article**
oder *Manchmal gehts auch ohne*

Sometimes, in certain expressions, the noun is used without any article at all:

Herr Giacobbe fährt gerne Zug. *Herr Giacobbe likes travelling by train.*
Frau Mozahebi ist Ingenieurin. *Frau Mozahebi is an engineer.*
Die neue Chefin hat nie Zeit. *The new boss never has any time.*

There is no article, for example, used with:

Proper names

Frau Bodet und Herr Merkle fahren nach München.
Frau Bodet and Herr Merkle are travelling to Munich.
Das ist Tina, meine Schwester.
That's Tina, my sister.

Occupations

Frau Syrova ist Programmiererin.
Frau Syrova is a computer programmer.

Nationalities

Robin Preuß ist Schweizer, Amir Mozahebi ist Deutscher.
Robin Preuß is Swiss, Amir Mozahebi is German.

Cities, (most) countries, continents

Unser Web-Designer kommt aus Indien.
Our web-designer comes from India.

Abstract ideas (sometimes)

Die Professorinnen kämpfen für Gleichberechtigung.
The female professors are fighting for equality.

Materials (sometimes)

Herr Radwan trinkt in der Kantine nie Bier.
Herr Radwan never drinks beer in the cantine.

Set phrases/idiomatic expressions

Die Reporterin holt tief Atem.
The reporter takes a deep breath.

Headlines and titles

Ministertreffen verschoben
Ministers' meeting postponed

Exercise 1

Complete the sentences with the definite or indefinite article or no article at all.

a) Herr Blum hat ....*eine*.... neue Assistentin.

....*Die*.... Assistentin kommt aus

.... Berlin.

b) Herr Bodet ist .... Marketingdirektor.

c) ....*das*.... alte Computerprogramm war

langsamer.

d) Frau Radwan fährt heute mit ihrem Kollegen nach

.... Hamburg.

e) Herr Stix ist .... Österreicher.

f) ....Der........... Kopierer ist schon wieder kaputt.

g) .... Tina macht einen Sprachkurs in

.... Spanien.

h) Während der Besprechung gab es nur

.... Kekse.

i) ......Die........... Kolleginnen im Callcenter müssen

.... Geduld aufbringen.

j) Die Sekretärin buchte ......einen..... Flug

nach Paris.

k) ......Der.......... Teamassistentin bestellt

......das plen...... Toner und ....das........... Papier.

l) Frau Kolar fand im Besprechungszimmer

......ein......... Handy.

m) Herr Hundt hat ......einen..... neuen Kollegen.

......Der......... Kollege kommt aus Leipzig.

n) Frau Danz schreibt ...einen.... Bericht.

......Der......... Bericht muss morgen fertig sein.

o) Hat .....die...... Firma .....ein......... Website?

Nein, die Firma hat wirklich ...eine..... Website.

2 Substantive Nouns
oder *Was ist das?*

die Mutter
the mother

der Vater
the father

die Großmutter
the grandmother

der Sohn
the son

der Hund
the dog

der Großvater
the grandfather

das Baby
the baby

die Tochter
the daughter

Nouns are used to give names to people, objects and things, as well as abstract ideas and are always written with a capital letter in German:

der **F**rieden, der **F**reund	*peace, friend*
die **K**atze, die **R**ose	*cat, rose*
das **H**aus, das **K**leid	*house, dress*

2.1 Genus Gender
oder *Aller guten Dinge sind drei*

In German every noun has a grammatical gender. The gender is shown by the article in front of the noun:

masculine	neuter	feminine
der Baum *tree*	**das** Handy *mobile phone*	**die** Blume *flower*
der Fluss *river*	**das** Mädchen *girl*	**die** Frau *woman*

The grammatical gender of a noun and the biological gender are usually the same:

masculine	feminine
der Mann, **der** Kollege	**die** Frau, **die** Kollegin
man, (male) colleague	*woman, (female) colleague*

But there are exceptions:

neuter
das Mädchen *girl*, **das** Kind *child*

Otherwise the choice of grammatical gender for a noun does not follow a logical set of rules. Luckily, there are a few simple rules applying to certain kinds of nouns that can help you remember.

• Masculine are:

Male persons, male jobs/occupations	
der Onkel, der Vater	*uncle, father*
der Ingenieur, der Grafiker	*(male) engineer, (male) designer*

Days of the week, months, seasons	
der Montag, der Dienstag	*Monday, Tuesday*
der Januar, der Februar	*January, February*
der Frühling, der Sommer	*spring, summer*

Most nouns with the following endings

-and/-ant	der Doktor**and**, der Prakti**ant** *doctoral candidate, trainee*
-ent	der Stud**ent**, der Pati**ent** *student, patient*
-er	der Comput**er**, der Besuch**er** *computer, visitor*
-ig	der Ess**ig**, der Hon**ig** *vinegar, honey*
-ismus	der Tour**ismus**, der Terror**ismus** *tourism, terrorism*
-ist	der Spezial**ist**, der Poliz**ist** *specialist, policeman*
-ling	der Früh**ling**, der Lehr**ling** *spring, apprentice*
-or	der Mot**or**, der Reakt**or** *motor, reactor*

• Neuter are:

Many nouns with the prefix Ge- at the beginning

das **Ge**müse, das **Ge**birge   *vegetables, mountains*

The infinitive forms of verbs acting as nouns

das Essen, das Rauchen   *eating, smoking*

All diminutive forms of nouns ending in

-chen	das Mäd**chen**, das Bröt**chen** *girl, bread roll*
-lein	das Büch**lein**, das Ring**lein** *little book, little ring*

A lot of nouns ending in

-nis	das Verzeich**nis**, das Geheim**nis** *register, secret*
-ment	das Medika**ment**, das Instru**ment** *medicine, instrument*
-o	das Bür**o**, das Aut**o** *office, car*
-t(r)um	das Wachs**tum**, das Stadtzen**trum** *growth, town centre*

- Feminine are:

Female persons, female jobs/occupations

die Tante, die Kollegin	*aunt, (female) colleague*
die Anwältin, die Architektin	*(female) lawyer, (female) architect*

Many flowers and trees

die Rose, die Tanne	*rose, fir tree*

Most nouns ending in

-ei	die Bücher**ei**, die Part**ei** *library, party*
-enz	die Konfer**enz**, die Exist**enz** *conference, existence*
-heit	die Frei**heit**, die Gesund**heit** *freedom, health*
-keit	die Möglich**keit**, die Geschwindig**keit** *possibility, speed*
-ie	die Industr**ie**, die Demokrat**ie** *industry, democracy*
-ik	die Fabr**ik**, die Polit**ik** *factory, politics*
-in	die Chef**in**, die Trainer**in** *(female) boss, (female) trainer*
-ion	die Reg**ion**, die Nat**ion** *region, nation*
-schaft	die Wirt**schaft**, die Wissen**schaft** *economy, science*
-tät	die Quali**tät**, die Produktivi**tät** *quality, productivity*
-ung	die Einlad**ung**, die Vertret**ung** *invitation, stand-in*

Exercise 2

Please add the correct article to these nouns.

die Freundschaft, *das* Häuschen, *der* Zwilling,

der Katalysator, *die* Freiheit, *die* Erziehung,

der/das Mechanismus, *die* Schülerin, *die/das* Musik,

das Brüderlein, *die* Verspätung, *die* Station,

der Präsident, *die* Biologie, *die* Kleinigkeit,

der Fabrikant, *der* König, *das* Radio,

die Verwandtschaft, *das* Visum, *der* Winter,

der Chef, *das* Instrument, *die* Druckerei,

die Universität, *das* Mädchen, *die/das* Sortiment

2.2 Singular und Plural   Singular and Plural
oder *Mehr als eins*

Nenne mir fünf Tiere in Afrika.

Zwei Löwen und drei Elefanten.

Give me five animals which live in Afrika. – Two lions and three elephants.

Normally every noun has a singular and a plural form. The accompanying article has to indicate this. Fortunately, in the plural the definite article is always the same – it doesn't matter whether the noun in the singular is masculine, neuter or feminine, the article in the plural is always die. The indefinite article in the plural is even easier: there isn't any (▷ p. 16).

The following table will help you to remember:

der/ein Mann	die/– Männer	man, men
das/ein Kind	die/– Kinder	child, children
die/eine Frau	die/– Frauen	woman, women

You have to remember, of course, that as a general rule nouns change their form in the plural. The following table shows you the different ways in which this can happen.

	singular	plural	plural ending	applies to
1 a	der Löffel	die Löffel	–	many nouns
	spoon	*spoons*		ending in
	das Zeichen	die Zeichen		**-el**, **-en**, **-er**,
	sign	*signs*		**-chen**, **-lein**
	das Messer	die Messer		
	knife	*knives*		
	das Mädchen	die Mädchen		
	girl	*girls*		
	das Büchlein	die Büchlein		
	little book	*little books*		
1 b	der Vater	die Väter	–,	many nouns
	father	*fathers*	with **Umlaut**	ending in
	die Mutter	die Mütter		**-el**, **-en**, **-er**,
	mother	*mothers*		**-chen**, **-lein**

	singular	plural	plural ending	applies to
2 a	der Schuh *shoe*	die Schuhe *shoes*	-e	many nouns with only one syllable
2 b	der Sohn *son* der Baum *tree*	die Söhne *sons* die Bäume *trees*	-e with Umlaut	many nouns with only one syllable
3	die Tasche *bag* die Lehrerin *teacher*	die Taschen *bags* die Lehrerinnen *teachers*	-n -nen -e, -in	feminine nouns ending in
4 a	das Bild *picture* das Kind *child*	die Bilder *pictures* die Kinder *children*	-er	many nouns with only one syllable
4 b	das Haus *house* das Blatt *leaf*	die Häuser *houses* die Blätter *leaves*	-er with Umlaut	many nouns with only one syllable
5	das Auto *car* das Kino *cinema*	die Autos *cars* die Kinos *cinemas*	-s	many words from other languages

L! Always learn a noun together with its article and the plural form. For example: die Regel, Regeln *rule*, *rules*.

Exercise 3

Please add the correct plurals.

a) die Reise   die _Reisen_

b) das Video   die _Videos_

c) der Brief   die _Briefe_

d) die Kassette   die _Kassetten_

e) das Brötchen   die _Brötchen_

f) der Tag   die _Tage_ ~~Tage~~ _Tage_

g) der Bohrer   die _Bohrer_

h) die Brille   die _Brillen_

i) das Motorrad   die _Motorräder_

j) der Stift   die _Stifte_

k) der Trainee   die _Trainees_

l) das Jahr   die _Jahre_

m) die Sekretärin   die _Sekretärinnen_

n) das Zimmer   die _Zimmer_

o) der Drucker   die _Druckers_

2.3 Kasus   Case Endings
oder *Auf jeden Fall vier Fälle*

Unlike English, German has retained case endings for nouns indicating the grammatical role they play in a sentence. Without them the meaning of the sentence would be unclear. Nouns are used in four different "cases":

Nominativ nominative, Akkusativ accusative, Dativ dative and Genitiv genitive. Each case indicates the part a noun plays in a sentence: the subject, object etc. The case is determined by the verb or by prepositions.

Case	Role in the sentence	What to ask
nom.	subject; subject's complement	Wer?, Was?
	Herr Bräuer ist mein Vorgesetzter.	Who? What?
	Herr Bräuer is my superior.	
acc.	standard object (similar to direct object in some languages)	Wen?, Was?
		Who(m)? What?
	Frau Schmitt liest einen Bericht.	
	Frau Schmitt is reading a report.	
	after some prepositions	
	Das Protokoll ist für den Chef.	
	The minutes are for the boss.	
dat.	special object (similar to indirect object in some languages)	Wem?
		To whom?
	Die Pizza schmeckt mir. *I like this pizza.*	
	after some prepositions	
	Er nimmt sein Handy aus der Tasche.	
	He takes his mobile phone out of his pocket.	
gen.	shows mostly a possessive relationship, it is sometimes used after certain prepositions	Wessen?
		Whose?
	Das Büro meines Vaters.	
	My father's office.	
	Aufgrund des schlechten Wetters wurde das Fußballspiel verschoben.	
	Due to the bad weather the football match was postponed.	

☼ Normally, there is only one nominative in a sentence. In sentences containing the verbs sein *to be*, heißen *to be called*, bleiben *to stay, to remain*, werden *to become*, however, there can be more than one nominative.

Herr Lehmann **ist** ein guter Rechtsanwalt.
Herr Lehmann is a good solicitor.
Frau Latour **wird** sicher eine gute Juristin.
Frau Latour is sure to become a good lawyer.

Some verbs are always followed by the dative:
e.g. antworten *to answer,* danken *to thank,* helfen *to help.*

antworten	Frau Sanchez antwortet **dir**.
	Frau Sanchez will answer you.
helfen	Herr Graf hilft **der Verkaufsassistentin**.
	Herr Graf is helping the sales assistant.

It's best to learn these by heart. In the appendix you'll find a list of all the dative verbs (▶ p. 172 ff.).

Other verbs can take both an accusative and a dative object just like in English! (In English we can also form the dative by adding *to*!)

bringen	Herr Lechner bringt **dem Vorstand die Folien**.
	Herr Lechner takes the transparencies to the board members.
geben	Herr Mayer gibt **seinem Kollegen den Schlüssel**.
	Herr Mayer gives his colleague the key.

With these verbs the person is normally in the dative (dem Vorstand, seinem Kollegen) and the non-person or object in the accusative (die Folien, den Schlüssel). In the sentence the dative object always comes before the accusative object. If, however the accusative object is a pronoun, it comes first and the dative object second.

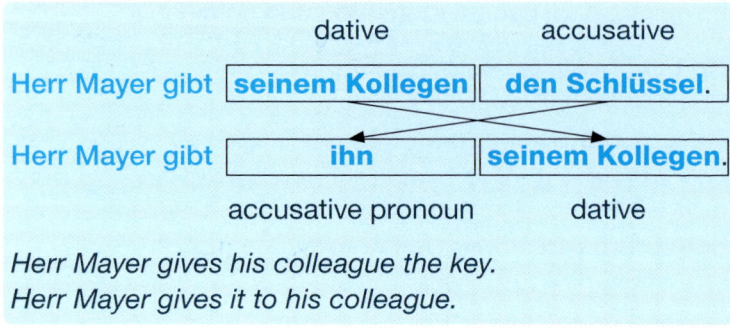

	dative	accusative
Herr Mayer gibt	**seinem Kollegen**	**den Schlüssel**.
Herr Mayer gibt	**ihn**	**seinem Kollegen**.
	accusative pronoun	dative

Herr Mayer gives his colleague the key.
Herr Mayer gives it to his colleague.

2.4   Deklination   Noun Declension
oder *Wer hilft dem Studenten?*

The different cases cause only a few changes to the endings of the nouns themselves.

	singular			plural
	masculine	neuter	feminine	
	the man	*the child*	*the woman*	*people*
nom.	der Mann	das Kind	die Frau	die Leute
acc.	den Mann	das Kind	die Frau	die Leute
dat.	dem Mann	dem Kind	der Frau	den Leute**n**
gen.	des Mann**es**	des Kind**es**	der Frau	der Leute

☼ For nouns in the singular the following rules apply:

- Feminine nouns remain the same in all cases.
- Masculine und neuter nouns in the genitive take the ending **-(e)s**.

- Nouns in the plural take an -n in the dative, unless they already end in -n or -s:

die Leute	mit den Leuten	*people, with the people*
die Frauen	mit den Frauen	*women, with the women*
die Autos	mit den Autos	*cars, with the cars*

Just to make things interesting, there are, of course, exceptions.
Several masculine nouns belong to the so-called n-declension, where in all cases except the nominative singular -(e)n is added:

	type A		type B	
nom.	der	Student	der	Name
acc.	den	Studenten	den	Namen
dat.	dem	Studenten	dem	Namen
gen.	des	Studenten	des	Namens
plural	die/den/der	Studenten	die/den/der	Namen

Don't worry: only very few nouns behave like this and they are all masculine except for one: Herz *heart*: das Herz (nom. and acc.), dem Herzen (dat.), des Herzens (gen.).

- Type A includes:

Male persons ending in -e	
der Junge	*boy*
der Kollege	*colleague*
der Franzose	*Frenchman*

Nouns that come from Latin or Greek ending in -ant, -at, -ent, -ist

der Diam**ant**	*diamond*
der Demokr**at**	*democrat*
der Stud**ent**	*student*
der Optim**ist**	*optimist*

• Type B includes:

A few abstract masculine nouns ending in -e

der Fried**e**	*peace*
der Gedank**e**	*thought*
der Nam**e**	*name*

Exercise 4

Please complete the following nouns by adding the correct endings where necessary.

a) Die Verkäuferin half dem Kunden..... bei der Suche.

b) Das ist mein Kollegen..... Martin.

c) Eine Redewendung besagt: Der Glaube......... versetzt Berge.

d) Herr Techmer hilft dem Praktikanten.... bei der Seminararbeit.

e) Die Richterin glaubt dem Zeugen...... .

f) Die Journalistin interviewt einen Experten...... .

g) Ich muss mich bei dem Lieferanten.... beschweren.

h) Der Höhepunkt ist die Ansprache des Bundespräsidenten... .

i) Die Fahndung nach dem Terroristen.... läuft auf Hochtouren.

j) Darüber machten wir uns keine Gedanken... .

3 Pronomen Pronouns
oder *Ich, du und die anderen*

> Du, raucht dein Pferd?
>
> Nein, wieso?
>
> Dann brennt dein Stall.

Hey you, does your horse smoke? – No why? – Well, than your barn's burning.

Pronouns are little words that often take the place of nouns or groups of nouns. They help us to avoid having to repeat things.

Milena kauft diesen Computer. *Milena is buying this computer.*
Sie kauft **ihn**. *She's buying it.*
Wem gehört diese Digitalkamera? *Who does this digital camera belong to?*
Das ist meine. *It's mine.*

Some pronouns, like the definite and indefinite articles, can also accompany a noun. These pronouns are called *Possessivartikel* in German. They have the same function as possessive adjectives (*my*, *your*, *his* etc.) in English.

Das ist mein Handy. *That's my mobile phone.*

These (adjectival) pronouns take on the gender, number and case of the noun that they stand for or describe.

3.1 Personalpronomen **Personal Pronouns**
oder *Ich und du*

Personal pronouns can replace a person, a noun or a group of nouns. Depending on their role in the sentence their form reflects the appropriate grammatical case.

Ich lese den Bericht. (nom.) *I'm reading the report.*
Möchtest **du** mit **uns** ins Kino gehen? (nom.; dat.)
Would you like to go to the cinema with us?
Der Assistent antwortet dem Abteilungsleiter.
The assistant answers the head of department.
Er antwortet **ihm**. (nom.; dat.) *He answers him.*

singular	1st person	2nd person	3rd person		
			masculine	neuter	feminine
nom.	ich	du	er	es	sie
acc.	mich	dich	ihn	es	sie
dat.	mir	dir	ihm	ihm	ihr
gen.	(meiner)	(deiner)	(seiner)	(seiner)	(ihrer)

plural	1st person	2nd person	3rd person	polite form
nom.	wir	ihr	sie	Sie
acc.	uns	euch	sie	Sie
dat.	uns	euch	ihnen	Ihnen
gen.	(unser/ unserer)	(euer/ eurer)	(ihrer)	(Ihrer)

⚡ We use the informal second person pronouns du (singular) and ihr (plural) when addressing children, good friends, family members or relations. Colleagues at work also often use the du/ihr form if they get on well together. The formal address pronoun Sie (both singular and plural) is used between strangers and adults who don't know each other well. It is also quite common for colleagues at work to use the Sie form even though they have known each other for years.

The formal and polite forms Sie/Ihnen remain the same in both the singular and the plural. They are always written with a capital letter.

The 3rd person singular pronoun has the same gender as the noun it stands for:

der: er	**Der Kollege** raucht. **Er** raucht.
	The colleague smokes. He smokes.
	Der Drucker läuft. **Er** läuft.
	The printer works. It works.

das: es	**Das Kind** weint. **Es** weint.
	The child is crying. He/She's crying.
	Das Telefon klingelt. **Es** klingelt.
	The telephone is ringing. It's ringing.

die: sie	**Die Chefin** kommt. **Sie** kommt.
	The boss is coming. She's coming.
	Die Tür geht auf. **Sie** geht auf.
	The door opens. It opens.

In the 3rd person plural no distinction in gender is necessary. The genitive case of the personal pronouns is very rarely used.

Exercise ⑤

Please complete the following sentences using the correct personal pronouns.

a) Mark arbeitet an einer neuen Homepage. Seit

.... sich mit Webdesign beschäftigt,

sieht man .... nur selten beim Joggen.

b) Julie sucht einen Job als Programmiererin.

.... hat auf diesem Gebiet bereits

Erfahrungen gesammelt.

c) Carlos geht ein Jahr nach Deutschland, um seine

Sprachkenntnisse zu verbessern. Es wird

.... dort bestimmt gefallen.

d) Hast .... daran gedacht, dass Andrea

heute eine Stelle als Praktikantin antritt?

.... solltest .... viel Glück

wünschen!

e) Herr Smith, ich danke ...., dass

.... gekommen sind.

f) Elena hat noch verschiedene Prüfungen zu absolvieren.

Wir werden .... dabei helfen.

g) Andrew, soll ich .... bei deiner Freundin

abholen?

3.2 Possessivartikel und -pronomen
Possessive Articles and Pronouns
oder *Alles meins!*

A possessive article indicates the person something belongs to:

Maria hat ein Handy. *Maria has got a mobile phone.*
Sie hat **ihr** Handy immer dabei. *She always has her mobile phone with her.*
Herr Romero sieht mit **seiner** neuen Brille besser aus als mit **seiner** alten. *Herr Romero's new glasses suit him better than his old ones.*
Meine Kollegin und ich haben einen Bericht über die Konferenz angefertigt. **Unser** Bericht ist im Intranet abrufbar. *My colleague and I have prepared a report on the conference. You can read our report on the intranet.*

The choice of possessive article is dictated by the person who possesses something:

ich	*I*	mein	*my*
du	*you*	dein	*your*
Sie	*you, formal*	Ihr	*your*
er	*he*	sein	*his*
es	*it*	sein	*its*
sie	*she*	ihr	*her*
wir	*we*	unser	*our*
ihr	*you, plural*	euer	*your*
sie	*they*	ihr	*their*
Sie	*you, plural, formal*	Ihr	*your*

Possessive articles follow the same formal rules as the indefinite article:

Das ist Simone und ihr Hund. *That's Simone and her dog.* (masculine, nom.)

Simone liebt ihren Hund. *Simone loves her dog.* (masculine, acc.)

Simone geht mit ihrem Hund zur Arbeit. *Simone goes to work with her dog.* (masculine, dat.)

⚡ There are two sides to every possessive article: the choice and the ending. The choice is determined by the person or the thing that possesses something and the ending by the noun and the role it plays in the sentence.

	singular			plural
	masculine	**neuter**	**feminine**	
	my computer	*my mobile phone*	*my camera*	*my things*
nom.	mein Computer	mein Handy	meine Kamera	meine Sachen
acc.	meinen Computer	mein Handy	meine Kamera	meine Sachen
dat.	meinem Computer	meinem Handy	meiner Kamera	meinen Sachen
gen.	meines Computers	meines Handys	meiner Kamera	meiner Sachen

Possessive pronouns on the other hand stand alone, i.e. they aren't followed by a noun.

Wem gehört der Ohrring? Das ist **meiner**. *Who does the earring belong to? It's mine.*
Sind das eure Folien? Nein, das sind nicht **unsere**. *Are those your transparencies? No, they're not ours.*

Possessive pronouns are declined in the same way as the definite article. They have the same endings (▷ **1.2** , p. 15):

	singular			plural
	masculine	neuter	feminine	
	der Wagen	*das Haus*	*die Jacht*	*die Sachen*
nom.	mein**er**	mein(e)**s**	mein**e**	mein**e**
acc.	mein**en**	mein(e)**s**	mein**e**	mein**e**
dat.	mein**em**	mein**em**	mein**er**	mein**en**

Deiner, seiner and ihrer are declined in the same way. Instead of unserer, unseres, unsere, euerer you'll often find unsrer, unsres, unsre, eurer. Possessive pronouns in the genitive are no longer used in normal speech.

There are several other pronouns that behave in the same way, i. e. they can stand alone without a noun and have the same endings as the definite article: irgendeiner, (irgend)welcher, jeder, (k)einer, mancher.

3.3 Demonstrativpronomen
Demonstrative Pronouns
oder *Dieses Buch*

Demonstrative pronouns show whether something is here or there. The following words can be used as demonstrative pronouns in German:

der, das, die *this/that*; dieser *this*; jener *that*; solcher *such*; derjenige *the one*; derselbe *the same*.

Dieses Briefing ist sehr informativ. *This briefing is very informative.*
Diese Bewerbung ist die interessanteste von allen. *This job application is the most interesting of all.*

In spoken language the definite article is often used as a demonstrative pronoun:

Welches Auto gefällt dir am besten? **Das** hier. *Which car do you like best? This one here.*
Kennst du den Kollegen da drüben? Ja, **den** kenne ich. *Do you know that colleague over there? Yes, I know him.*
Welches ist deine Tasse? **Die** da. *Which is your cup? That one there.*

- The forms are the same as those of the definite article except for the dative plural denen and the genitive dessen (masculine + neuter), derer (feminine + plural).

- The endings of the demonstrative pronouns dieser, jener, solcher are the same as those of the definite article:

	masculine	neuter	feminine	plural
nom.	dieser	dieses	diese	diese
acc.	diesen	dieses	diese	diese
dat.	diesem	diesem	dieser	diesen
gen.	dieses	dieses	dieser	dieser

- Both derjenige and derselbe are compound words. The first part follows the same rules as the definite article. The second part -jenige or -selbe changes as follows:

	masculine	neuter	feminine	plural
nom.	derjenige	dasjenige	diejenige	diejenigen
acc.	denjenigen	dasjenige	diejenige	diejenigen
dat.	demjenigen	demjenigen	derjenigen	denjenigen
gen.	desjenigen	desjenigen	derjenigen	derjenigen

Diejenigen, die mit den Aufgaben fertig sind, können hinausgehen. *Those of you who have finished the exercises can go out.*
Das war wieder dasselbe komische Geräusch wie gestern Abend. *That was the same funny noise as yesterday evening.*
Warum hörst du immer dieselbe Musik? *Why do you always listen to the same music?*

Exercise 6

Please complete the following sentences with the correct demonstrative pronouns dieser, diese, dieses, diesem and diesen.

a) Wer hat .... Film mit Julia Roberts gesehen?

b) .... CD-Player gehört Luca.

c) Wir wussten nicht, wie .... Diktiergerät funktionierte.

d) .... Verhalten gab mir zu denken.

e) Sie sollten .... Vorfall keine Beachtung schenken.

f) Ich habe .... Wort noch nie gehört.

g) .... Fragen wurden mithilfe des Internets gelöst.

h) Carla wird .... Wohnung in Hamburg mieten.

Exercise 7

Please put in the missing demonstrative pronouns.

Wir suchen Möbel für unsere Wohnung in Deutschland und finden in einem Einrichtungshaus …

a) … einen Küchentisch. – .... ist leider zu groß für unsere Küche.

b) … einen Einbauschrank. – .... gefällt uns ausgezeichnet.

c) … eine Eckbank. – .... ist uns zu teuer.

d) … Stühle für die Essecke. – .... können wir auf jeden Fall gebrauchen.

e) … einen Schreibtisch. – .... ist etwas zu klein.

f) … eine Wohnzimmerlampe. – .... sollten wir gleich mitnehmen.

3.4 Fragepronomen Interrogative Pronouns
oder *Wer denn, wo denn, was denn?*

What kind of pronouns do we use when asking questions? Look at the following examples and the words in bold print:

Wer hat angerufen? **Dr. Dorsch** hat gestern angerufen.
Who called? Dr Dorsch called yesterday.
Wen hast du getroffen? Ich habe gestern **Frau Richter** getroffen. *Who did you meet? I met Frau Richter yesterday.*
Was steht in der E-Mail? In der E-Mail steht **der Liefertermin**. *What was in the e-mail? The delivery date was in the e-mail.*

By using interrogative pronouns (or: w-question words) we can ask questions about different parts of a sentence. To ask about a person we use wer? and to ask about things we use was? They change their form according to case, depending on their grammatical role in the sentence.

	person	thing
nom.	wer?	was?
acc.	wen?	was?
dat.	wem?	was?
gen.	wessen?	wessen?

Interrogative pronouns are also used together with prepositions. Here, too, we have to distinguish between a person and a thing.

• If we ask about a person, we use a preposition followed by the interrogative pronoun in the appropriate case.

An wen denkst du gerade? Ich denke an meinen Freund. *Who are you thinking of? I'm thinking of my friend.*
Von wem spricht er? Er spricht von seinem Kollegen. *Who is he talking about? He's talking about his colleague.*

• If we ask about a thing, we use wo(r) + preposition.

Woran denkst du gerade? Ich denke an meinen Urlaub. *What are you thinking of at the moment? I'm thinking of my holiday.*
Wovon erzählt er? Er erzählt von seinem Wochenendausflug. *What's he talking about? He's talking about his weekend trip.*

Two more interrogative pronouns are welcher and was für ein. Just as possessive pronouns they can be used like an article with a noun or they can stand alone.

Welches Kleid gefällt dir am besten? *Which dress do you like best?*
Hier sind verschiedene Kleider. **Welches** gefällt dir am besten? *Here are several dresses. Which do you like best?*
Was für eine Jacke suchst du? *What kind of jacket are you looking for?*
Ich suche eine Lederjacke. *I'm looking for a leather jacket.*
Was für eine denn? *What kind then?*

☼ Welcher, used either as an article or a pronoun, is declined in the same way. It takes the same signal endings as the definite article (▶ **1.2** , p. 15). When using was für einer, remember that was für always remains the same and only einer changes.

Used as an article einer is declined in the same way as the indefinite article (▷ 1.2 , p. 15). Used as a pronoun einer is declined in the same way as the definite article and takes the same signal endings (▷ 1.2 , p. 15). Used as a pronoun einer cannot take the genitive form. For the plural form use the corresponding form of welcher instead of einer.

3.5 Reflexiv- und Reziprokpronomen
Reflexive and Reciprocal Pronouns
oder Ich freue mich …

Du siehst aber blass aus.

Ich habe mich gewaschen.

You're looking pale. – I just had a wash.

Here's some good news! Reflexive pronouns only occur in the accusative and dative. And apart from the 3rd person their forms are the same as the personal pronouns.

	accusative	dative
ich	mich	mir
du	dich	dir
er/es/sie	sich	sich
wir	uns	uns
ihr	euch	euch
sie/Sie	sich	sich

➡ There is a large number of verbs in German that require a reflexive pronoun. We call them reflexive verbs.

Er **bewirbt sich** um diese Stelle. *He's applying for this job.*
Sie hat **sich** leider **erkältet.** *Unfortunately, she's caught a cold.*

L! Always remember the reflexive pronoun when learning reflexive verbs (sich bewerben, sich erkälten …)!

There are also verbs that sometimes have a reflexive pronoun and sometimes don't, depending on their meaning.

Anne **wäscht** den Pullover. *Anne is washing the pullover.*
Julian **wäscht sich** die Hände. *Julian is washing his hands.*
Frau Böttcher **versteckt** das Geschenk. *Frau Böttcher hides the present.*
Die Kinder **verstecken sich** im Schrank. *The children hide in the cupboard.*

Reciprocal pronouns are used to express a two-way relationship between people or things. They correspond to the English *each other* or *one another*.

Harry Richter und Lisa Mayer **lieben sich** (oder: einander). *Harry Richter and Lisa Mayer love each other.* Die beiden Brüder **helfen sich** (gegenseitig). *The two brothers help each other.*

The reciprocal pronoun -einander is also used in combination with prepositions.

Die Akten liegen alle **übereinander.** *The files are lying on top of one another.* Kathrin und Mary haben viel **voneinander** gelernt. *Kathrin and Mary have learned a lot from each other.*

Exercise 8

Please put in the correct reflexive and reciprocal pronouns.

a) Lars kauft .... ein neues Sweatshirt.

b) Ich freue .... über das bestandene Zertifikat.

c) Die Polizei interessierte .... für den Vorfall.

d) Frau Glück und Herr Wein helfen ....

e) Alexander putzt .... die Zähne.

f) Wir machten .... über den Jahresabschluss Gedanken.

g) Die Kontoauszüge lagen durch............................ auf dem Tisch.

h) Heute gehen wir mit .... ins Kino.

4 Adjektive Adjectives
oder *Schön und jung*

Fresh Milk

Adjectives are used to describe, characterise or modify people and things – in grammatical terms they qualify nouns.

4.1 Adjektivendungen Adjectival Endings
oder *Ende gut, alles gut*

Adjectives are easiest to use in German when they come after the noun because they remain in their basic form and don't change their endings.

> Das Zimmer ist **schön**. *The room is nice.*
> Der Discjockey ist **jung**. *The disc jockey is young.*

Things become much more interesting, however, when the adjective stands before the noun. Here it takes on different endings: it has to be declined.

> Herr Radwan bestellt einen französisch**en** Wein. *Herr Radwan orders some French wine.*
> Der französisch**e** Wein schmeckt ihm. *The French wine tastes good.*
> Frau Radwan isst Apfelstrudel mit heiß**er** Vanillesoße. *Frau Radwan is eating apple strudel with hot custard.*

It's not too difficult to get the endings for the adjective right. They are determined by

- the article in front of the adjective and its signal ending
- the gender, number and case of the noun that follows

The following table will help you to remember:

der trocken**e** Wein	*the dry wine*
article *with* signal ending	
noun: masculine, singular, nom.	
ein trocken**er** Wein	*a dry wine*
article *without* signal ending	
noun: masculine, singular, nom.	

Now there are just two more rules for us to learn:

- If the adjective is preceded by an article with a signal ending, then the adjective takes the ending -e oder -en (der trockene Wein).

	masculine	neuter	feminine	plural
nom.	-e	-e	-e	-en
acc.	-en	-e	-e	-en
dat.	-en	-en	-en	-en
gen.	-en	-en	-en	-en

- If the adjective is preceded by an article without a signal ending (▷ **1.2** , p. 15) or if there is no article at all, then the adjective itself is required to provide the necessary signal ending. Usually an -e- is added between the basic form of the adjective and the signal ending: trockener Wein.

To remind you, here again is a list of the signal endings:

	masculine	neuter	feminine	plural
nom.	r	s	e	e
acc.	n	s	e	e
dat.	m	m	r	n
gen.	s	s	r	r

In context the result is as follows:

	masculine	neuter	feminine	plural
	the/a dry wine	*the/a cold beer*	*the/a warm milk*	*the/– good drinks*
nom.	der trockene Wein	das kühle Bier	die warme Milch	die guten Getränke
nom.	ein trockener Wein	ein kühles Bier	eine warme Milch	gute Getränke
nom.	trockener Wein	kühles Bier	warme Milch	gute Getränke
acc.	den trockenen Wein	das kühle Bier	die warme Milch	die guten Getränke
acc.	einen trockenen Wein	ein kühles Bier	eine warme Milch	gute Getränke
acc.	trockenen Wein	kühles Bier	warme Milch	gute Getränke
dat.	dem trockenen Wein	dem kühlen Bier	der warmen Milch	den guten Getränken
dat.	einem trockenen Wein	einem kühlen Bier	einer warmen Milch	guten Getränken
dat.	trockenem Wein	kühlem Bier	warmer Milch	guten Getränken
gen.	des trockenen Weines	des kühlen Bieres	der warmen Milch	der guten Getränke
gen.	eines trockenen Weines	eines kühlen Bieres	einer warmen Milch	guter Getränke
gen.	trockenen Weines	kühlen Bieres	warmer Milch	guter Getränke

The table shows how the signal endings can jump, as it were, between article and adjective.

⚡ The endings in the genitive masculine and neuter without an article are an exception. They differ from the expected signal endings and have -en instead. The signal ending jumps over to the noun. These forms do not occur very often though.

The two adjectives lila and rosa don't take any kind of ending:

Sie trägt eine **rosa** Bluse mit **lila** Streifen. *She's wearing a pink blouse with purple stripes.*

Exercise 9
Please complete the following sentences by adding the correct endings to the adjectives.

a) Mit diesem Management wird das Unternehmen nie auf einen grün......... Zweig kommen.

b) Alicée will immer die erst......... Geige spielen.

c) Maria ist gerade noch einmal mit einem blau......... Auge davongekommen.

d) Hier geht doch etwas nicht mit recht......... Dingen zu.

e) Wir sollten das nicht an die groß......... Glocke hängen.

f) Mike wurde mit offen......... Armen empfangen.

g) An dieser Aufführung hat der Theaterkritiker kein gut......... Haar gelassen.

h)   Vor diesem Vorhaben hat er kalt......... Füße.

i)   Das Ereignis traf uns wie ein Blitz aus heiter.........

Himmel!

j)   Dies sollte man nicht auf die leicht......... Schulter

nehmen.

Each of these sentences contains a very useful idiomatic phrase for you to learn by heart. The translation can be found with the answer key in the appendix.

4.2   Steigerung der Adjektive
Comparison of Adjectives
oder *Schnell, schneller, am schnellsten*

In this age of rapid change and fierce competition the need to compare things is growing. In grammatical terms we can do this by using the positive, comparative and superlative forms of the adjective.

• Positive:

Das Mofa ist schnell. *The moped is fast.*
Mein Motorrad ist so schnell wie deins. *My motorbike is as fast as yours.*
Das schnelle Mofa gehört diesem Jungen. *The fast moped belongs to this boy.*

• Comparative: + -er

Das Motorrad ist schneller als das Mofa. *The motorbike is faster than the moped.*
Das schnellere Motorrad hat gewonnen. *The faster motorbike has won.*

- Superlative: + (e)sten

> **Das Flugzeug ist am schnellsten.** *The aeroplane is fastest.*
> **Wir fliegen im schnellsten Flugzeug der Welt.** *We're flying in the fastest aeroplane in the world.*

When do adjectives in the comparative and superlative have different adjectival endings and when do they not? Here the same rules apply as for the normal form.

- If the adjective comes after the noun, then it doesn't change:

> **Das Motorrad ist schneller als das Mofa.** *The motorbike is faster than the moped.*
> **Das Flugzeug ist am schnellsten.** *The aeroplane is fastest.*

- The adjective takes on different endings if it stands before the noun:

> **Das schnellere Motorrad hat gewonnen.** *The faster motorbike has won.*
> **Wir fliegen im schnellsten Flugzeug der Welt.** *We're flying in the fastest aeroplane in the world.*

☼ All three forms (positive, comparative and superlative) can come before or after the noun and they all obey the same rules as far as the endings are concerned.

- There are, however, one or two special cases. The ending in the superlative is -esten if the adjective ends with -d, -s, -ss, -ß, -sch, -t, -tz, -x, or -z and the emphasis is on the final syllable:

gesund	gesünder	am gesünd**esten**
healthy	*healthier*	*healthiest*
schlecht	schlechter	am schlecht**esten**
bad	*worse*	*worst*
hübsch	hübscher	am hübsch**esten**
pretty	*prettier*	*prettiest*
stolz	stolzer	am stolz**esten**
proud	*prouder*	*proudest*

- In lots of cases a, o, u change to ä, ö, ü, e.g.:

kalt	kälter	am kältesten
cold	*colder*	*coldest*
groß	größer	am größten
big	*bigger*	*biggest*
klug	klüger	am klügsten
clever	*cleverer*	*cleverest*

- Other irregular forms are:

gut	besser	am besten
good	*better*	*best*
viel	mehr	am meisten
much	*more*	*most*
hoch	höher	am höchsten
high	*higher*	*highest*
nah	näher	am nächsten
near	*nearer*	*nearest*
teuer	teurer	am teuersten
dear	*dearer*	*dearest*
dunkel	dunkler	am dunkelsten
dark	*darker*	*darkest*

Exercise ⑩
Please complete the following sentences with the correct form of the adjective: positive, comparative or superlative.

a) groß:

Eileen ist so .... wie Pia.

Pia ist .... als Marcus.

Tom ist von allen Praktikanten ....

b) gut:

Herr Porter spricht so .... Deutsch wie

Frau Hundt.

Frau Hundt spricht .... Deutsch als Sarah.

Gina spricht .... Deutsch.

c) gesund:

Limonade ohne Zucker ist ....

Apfelschorle ist allerdings ....·

Und ein Glas Wein am Abend ist ....·

d) viel:

Über naturwissenschaftliche Erkenntnisse wusste

Inka ....

Über technische Neuerungen noch ....

Und über sprachliche Angelegenheiten

....

5 Adverbien und Modalpartikel
Adverbs and Modal Particles
oder *Gestern und eigentlich*

5.1 Adverbien   Adverbs
oder *Es kommt auf das Wie an*

Adverbs describe how, where, when, where to, where from, how long or why something happens. The good news: Adverbs never need to be declined! And many adverbs have the same form, the same comparative and superlative forms as adjectives.

- Adverbs of Location/Place

draußen *outside*	**Bei diesem schönen Wetter essen wir draußen.** *The weather is so nice we can eat outside.*
nirgends *nowhere/* *not … anywhere*	**Ich kann meine Brille nirgends finden.** *I can't find my glasses anywhere.*

- Adverbs of Direction

dahin there/ in that direction	Er läuft **dahin**. *He's running there.*
hinauf up	Die Kinder klettern den Baum **hinauf**. *The children climb up the tree.*

- Adverbs of Time

heute today	**Heute** habe ich leider keine Zeit. *I don't have time today, I'm afraid.*
meistens mostly/usually	Wenn Mona in die Stadt fährt, parkt sie **meistens** im Parkhaus. *When Mona drives into town, she usually parks in the multi-storey carpark.*

- Adverbs of Manner

leider unfortunately	Frank kann **leider** nicht mit ins Konzert kommen. *Frank can't come with us to the concert unfortunately.*
langsam slowly	Es ist gesund, **langsam** zu essen. *It's healthy to eat slowly.*

- Adverbs of Cause

They can be used as a replacement for conjunctions.

trotzdem nevertheless	Es regnet. **Trotzdem** mache ich jetzt einen Spaziergang. *It's raining. Nevertheless I'm going for a walk.*
deshalb for that reason	Marias Eltern wohnen in Kanada. **Deshalb** fliegt sie jedes Jahr dorthin. *Maria's parents live in Canada. She flies there every year for that reason.*

Adverbs form only a very small part of German grammar. They are no more than simple vocabulary items. Is that all we have to remember? Well, no. Not quite. There are a few irregular comparative and superlative forms that you need to learn. Here they are:

bald	eher	am ehesten
soon	*sooner*	*soonest*
gern	lieber	am liebsten
gladly	*rather/preferably*	*most of all*
oft	öfter/häufiger	am häufigsten
often	*more often*	*most often*
viel	mehr	am meisten
much	*more*	*most of all*

Where do we put adverbs in a sentence?

• Directly after a verb:

Sie singt **schön**. *She sings beautifully.*

• Alongside a noun:

Das Konzert **gestern** war fantastisch. *The concert yesterday was fantastic.*

• With an adjective:

Dieser Film ist **ziemlich** spannend. *The film is rather exciting.*

• At the very beginning:

Gestern war das Konzert fantastisch. (for emphasis) *Yesterday the concert was fantastic.*

Even whole phrases can be used as adverbs:

Sie singt **schön**. *She sings beautifully.*
Sie singt **hier**. *She's singing here.*
Sie singt **in der Oper**. *She's singing in the opera.*

And what do we do when there are several adverbs or adverbial expressions in one sentence? Where do we put them all? In what order or sequence? A useful rule of thumb is: **T**ime – **C**ause – **M**anner and **L**ocation/Place. But if a certain part of the sentence needs to be emphasised, it can be placed elsewhere.

Er arbeitet heute (Time) wegen der kommenden Prüfung (Cause) fieberhaft (Manner) in der Bibliothek (Location/Place). *He's working today feverishly in the library because of the impending exam.*
Wegen der kommenden Prüfung arbeitet er heute fieberhaft in der Bibliothek. *Because of the impending exam he's working feverishly in the library today.*

L! Think of a **T**ea-drinking **CaMeL**!

5.2 Modalpartikel **Modal Particles**
oder *Aber eigentlich vielleicht doch*

Modal particles add a little spice to the language.
Modal particles are used in spoken language to express
feelings, emotions and subjective views. The same particles used in different contexts and with different emphasis can have different meanings.

Da bist du **ja**! *There you are!*

possible meanings:
Ich freue mich, dass du da bist. *I'm glad you're here.*
Ich ärgere mich, dass ich auf dich warten musste.
I'm annoyed at having had to wait for you.

Peter: Willst du mit ins Kino?
Peter: *Do you want to come to the cinema with me?*
Alan: **Eigentlich** müsste ich für meine Prüfung lernen.
Alan: *Actually, I ought to be studying for my exam.*

possible meanings:
Ich habe keine Lust zu lernen, fühle mich aber
verpflichtet. *I don't really want to study, but I feel I must.*
Ich will lieber lernen, aber ich will dich auch nicht
enttäuschen. *I'd prefer to study, but I don't want to
disappoint you.*

Was liest du **denn** da? *What's that you're reading?*
possible meanings:
Ich interessiere mich für das, was du liest. *I'm interested
in what you're reading.*
Ich ärgere mich darüber, dass du etwas liest, weil du
etwas anderes tun solltest. *I'm annoyed that you're
reading when you should be doing something else.*

Here are some other modal particles in common use:

modal particle	example	possible meaning
aber	Das ist aber gut! *That's really good!*	You're surprised.
bloß	Was hast du denn bloß? *What ever is the matter?*	You're emphasising your feelings. Here: worry.
denn	Wie heißt du denn? *So what's your name?*	You're showing interest.
eben	Das ist eben das Leben. *That's life, isn't it?*	You're emphasising your feelings. Here: resignation.
etwa	Sind die Entwürfe etwa noch nicht fertig? *Don't tell me the designs aren't ready yet!*	You're showing amazement or annoyance.
halt	Hans ist halt so. *Hans just happens to be like that.*	You're emphasing your emotions. Here: resignation.
mal	Halte das bitte mal für mich. *Hold that for me a minute, would you?*	Friendly request.
nur	Ich wollte ja nur fragen. *I was only asking.*	You want to justify yourself.
schon	Das wird schon richtig sein so. *That'll be OK as it is.*	You confirm a previous statement and show no further interest.
wohl	Das Paket wird wohl morgen eingehen. *The parcel will arrive tomorrow, I expect.*	You're expressing an assumption.

L! The best way to learn modal particles is to learn them in context. Listen carefully to native speakers of German as much as possible and make a note of how they use these little words in everyday speech.

Exercise ⑪
Please complete the following sentences using one of the modal particles in brackets.

a) Das habe ich mir (denn/eben/nur) ....

vorgenommen.

b) Daran hat Vivian in der Eile (etwa/halt/mal)

.... nicht mehr gedacht.

c) Wo habe ich (bloß/aber/schon) ....

meine Uhr hingelegt?

d) Was ist (vielleicht/eben/denn) .... hier

los?

e) Das ist (wohl/aber/bloß) .... großzügig

von Ihnen!

f) Genau das habe ich (mal/etwa/doch)

.... gerade befürchtet!

g) Andy hat das (wohl/mal/etwa) .... nicht

so ernst genommen.

h) Dies konnte ich mir (eben/ja/bloß) ....

denken!

6 Wortstellung Word Order
oder *Was kommt wann*

Warum kochst du immer Gulasch? Koch doch mal was anderes!

Ich koche immer was anderes! Es wird aber immer Gulasch.

Why are you always cooking goulash? Cook something else once in a while! – I do cook something different every day. But it always turns out a goulash.

Word order in German is much more liberal than in English. But there are one or two rules that are uniquely German.

The most important of these is the position of the verb or verbs in a sentence. The word order varies depending on whether you're forming a statement, a question with an interrogative pronoun, a question without an interrogative pronoun, an imperative or a subordinate clause.

- Statement Aussagesatz

Er **liest** das Protokoll. *He's reading the minutes.*

- Question with Interrogative Pronoun
  Fragesatz mit Fragewort

Was **liest** er? *What is he reading?*

- Question without Interrogative Pronoun
  Fragesatz ohne Fragewort

Liest er wirklich das Protokoll? *Is he really reading the minutes?*

- Imperative Imperativ

Kommen Sie bitte sofort! *Please come at once.*

- Subordinate Clause Nebensatz

Ich weiß, dass er das Protokoll **liest**. *I know that he's reading the minutes.*

In statements, the main inflected verb always comes in second place. The subject is placed as close as possible to the verb, either immediately before or after it. If there are several verbs in the sentence or uninflected parts of verbs like infinitives or participles, these always go to the end, thus forming a kind of verbal bracket around the rest of the sentence.

position 1	position 2 (inflected verb)	middle (variable number of elements)	end (other verbs or parts of verbs)
Alan	beginnt	heute sein Praktikum bei BMW in München.	
Heute	beginnt	Alan sein Praktikum bei BMW in München.	
Wann	beginnt	Alan sein Praktikum bei BMW in München?	
Heute	fängt	das Praktikum von Alan bei BMW in München	an.
Gestern	hat	das Praktikum von Alan bei BMW in München	angefangen.
Wo	hat	Alan gestern ein Praktikum	angefangen?
Alan	hätte	gestern sein Praktikum bei BMW in München	anfangen sollen.

Alan begins his work programme at BMW in Munich today.
Today Alan begins his work programme at BMW in Munich.
When does Alan begin his work programme at BMW in Munich?
Today Alan's work programme at BMW in Munich starts.
Yesterday Alan's work programme at BMW in Munich started.
Where did Alan start his work programme yesterday?
Alan should have started his work programme at BMW in Munich yesterday.

In questions, on the other hand, the sentence starts immediately with the verb:

inflected verb	middle	end (other verbs or parts of verbs)
Fängst	du morgen dein Praktikum	an?
Hat	dein Praktikum schon	begonnen?
Gehst	du mit uns heute Abend ins Kino?	

Are you starting your work programme tomorrow?
Has your work programme already started?
Are you going to the cinema with us this evening?

In subordinate clauses all verbs and parts of verbs come at the end:

main clause	subordinate clause	verbs in the sub-ordinate clause	main clause
Ich freue mich,	dass du	gekommen bist.	
	Weil du Filme so	magst,	wollten wir dich heute Abend ins Kino einladen.
Er fragt sich,	welches Handy er	kaufen soll.	
	Sobald ich	angekommen bin,	werde ich euch anrufen.

I'm glad you've come.
Because you like films so much, we wanted to invite you to come with us to the cinema this evening.
He's wondering which mobile phone he should buy.
As soon as I've arrived, I'll call you.

If the main clause follows the subordinate clause, it starts immediately with the verb since the subordinate clause has taken over first position in the sentence instead of the main clause.

position 1	position 2 (inflected verb)	middle	end (other parts of verbs)
Sobald ich angekommen bin, werde		ich euch	anrufen.
As soon as I've arrived, I'll call you.			

Now you know the most important rules for word order in German sentences. The various elements in the middle part of a sentence can be ordered in different ways. You'll learn about these in each individual chapter of this book (▷ **2.3** on p. 29 ff., **5.1** on p. 60 ff.).

Exercise 12
Please change the word order in the following sentences and start with the part in bold print.

a) Hardy hat am Montag eine Agenda für das nächste Meeting erhalten.

....

b) Rebecca hat dieses Geschenk von ihrem Mann bekommen.

....

c) Die Touristen nehmen um 10:30 Uhr an einer Stadtführung teil.

....

d) Yvonne hat heute einen Termin in der Autowerkstatt.

....

e) Frau Simon hätte den Gesprächstermin wahrnehmen sollen.

....

f) Margarita fährt mit dem Bus in die Stadt.

....

Exercise 13
Please turn the following statements into questions.

a) Ich gehe heute Abend mit Muriel in die Stadt.

....

b) Wir besuchen am Wochenende meine Cousine.

....

c) Am Samstag muss ich mich auf das Bewerbungs-gespräch vorbereiten.

....

d) Wir treffen uns heute Nachmittag auf einen Kaffee.

....

e) Ich beschäftige mich gerade mit den Regeln der deutschen Grammatik.

....

f) Das Training hat bereits begonnen.

....

7 Verben Verbs
oder *Was alles passiert*

> **Wenn die Lampe nicht brennt, musst du absteigen und schieben.**

> **Das habe ich schon gemacht, aber dann brennt sie auch nicht.**

You have to dismount and push your bike if the lamp doesn't work. – I tried that already but it still doesn't work.

We are now going to take you on a journey through the wonderful world of verbs, a story with many chapters. In German, verbs play an especially important role in a variety of ways. On the one hand, just as in English, they define and provide meaning to an important part of any sentence: verbs tell us what someone does or what happens. In a grammatical sense the verb is king: it always takes up a specially reserved position in the sentence (▷ p. 67) and it "rules" by determining the case of the nouns (▷ **2.3** , p. 29).

Verbs, too, can change their form (conjugation). They change according to:

• Person

> ich lese; du liest; er liest; wir lesen usw.
> *I read; you read; he reads; we read etc.*

- Tense

> ich lese heute; ich las gestern …
> *I am reading today; I was reading yesterday …*

- Mood (Indicative/Subjunctive)

> ich lese (wirklich); ich lese jetzt nicht, aber ich würde (gerne) lesen
> *I am (actually) reading; I am not reading now, but I would (like to) read*

- Voice (Active/Passive)

> Ich lese diese Fachzeitschrift jede Woche.
> *I read this magazine every week.*
> Diese Fachzeitschrift wird von vielen gelesen.
> *This magazine is read by many people.*

Fortunately, the different forms can often be recognized by the endings that are added to the main verb stem depending on the person. These are the endings:

regular endings	
ich	–
du	-st
er/es/sie	–
wir	-en
ihr	-t
sie/Sie	-en

In the present indicative the ending for ich (singular) is: -e and the ending for er, es, sie is -t. Exceptions are the modal verbs and the verb sein *to be*.

Here are two examples:

	simple past	present
ich	schrieb- –	schreib-**e**
du	schrieb-**st**	schreib-**st**
er/es/sie	schrieb- –	schreib-**t**
wir	schrieb-**en**	schreib-**en**
ihr	schrieb-**t**	schreib-**t**
sie/Sie	schrieb-**en**	schreib-**en**
	stem + ending	stem + ending

⚡ Two identical sounds are combined into one.
E. g.: wir sag-te-en becomes **sag-te-n** (first person plural simple past).

The basic form of the verb, the infinitive, never changes and always ends in -en: schreiben *to write,* sagen *to say,* wissen *to know.* Exception: sein *to be*

There are, however, several quite different types of verbs in German … but let's not rush things. We'll deal with them all in turn.

7.1 Hilfsverben Auxiliary Verbs
oder *Sein, haben und werden*

The three verbs sein, haben and werden can either be independent main verbs in their own right, or they can help out other verbs in an auxiliary function to form the different tenses of those verbs:

Vanessa **hat** Boxhandschuhe. *Vanessa has some boxing-gloves.*
= **haben** as a main verb

Vanessa **hat** Boxhandschuhe **gekauft**. *Vanessa has bought some boxing-gloves.*
= **haben** as an auxiliary forming the perfect tense of **kaufen**

Herr Gabor **ist** Rechtsanwalt. *Herr Gabor is a solicitor.*
= **sein** as a main verb

Herr Vollmer **ist** zu einem Rechtsanwalt **gegangen**. *Herr Vollmer has gone to a solicitor.*
= **sein** as an auxiliary forming the perfect tense of **gehen**

Carmen **wird** Informatikerin. *Carmen is going to be a computer expert.*
= **werden** as a main verb

Die Datei **wird gespeichert**. *The file is being saved.*
= **werden** as an auxiliary forming the present tense passive of **speichern**

These three verbs are exceptional also in the way they are conjugated. Their present tense forms are as follows:

	sein	**haben**	**werden**
ich	bin	hab-**e**	werd-**e**
du	bi-**st**	ha-**st**	wir-**st**
er/es/sie	is-**t**	ha-**t**	wir-**d**
wir	sind	hab-**en**	werd-**en**
ihr	seid	hab-**t**	werd-**et**
sie/Sie	sind	hab-**en**	werd-**en**

Remember that in German there are no continuous or progressive forms of the verb. Unlike English, the continuous aspect can be expressed by the simple form. The translations given here reflect this, depending on the meaning and the context.

7.2 Modalverben Modal Verbs
oder *Müsste ich können*

Modal verbs are normally used in combination with the infinitive of a main verb. They describe the way or the manner in which things happen and often reflect the personal attitude or perspective of the speaker. Thus, the same modal verb can often have a variety of meanings.

Sie **kann** sehr schön **singen**. *She can sing most beautifully.*
= ability
Kannst du mir mal **helfen**? *Can you help me?*
= friendly request
Hier **darf** man nicht **rauchen**. *You're not allowed to smoke here.*
= (no) permission
Er **muss** den Bericht heute Abend abgeben. *He's got to deliver the report this evening.*
= obligation

The following table shows the various meanings modal verbs can have:

dürfen	permission	Sie **dürfen** hier parken. *You can/may park here.*
	politeness	**Darf** ich Ihnen meinen neuen Assistenten vorstellen? *May I introduce my new assistent?*
	presumption	Die Besprechung **dürfte** um 10 Uhr beendet sein. *The meeting should be over at 10 o'clock.*
nicht dürfen	permission denied	In der Kantine **darf** man nicht rauchen. *You are not allowed to smoke in the cantine.*

können	friendly request	**Können** Sie mich mit Frau Aristov verbinden? *Can you put me through to Frau Aristov?*
	possibility	Herr Bari hat Zeit und **kann** Frau Kundera vom Flughafen abholen. *Herr Bari has got time and can pick up Frau Kundera from the airport.*
	ability	Oliver **kann** problemlos einen Marathon laufen. *Oliver can run the marathon without any problem.*
	permission	Sie **können** den Dienstwagen nehmen. *You can take the firm's car.*
mögen	to like/love	Linda **mag** Schokoladeneis. *Linda likes chocolate ice cream.*
„**möchte**"	wish	Paula **möchte** einmal nach Südafrika reisen. *Paula would like to travel to South Africa.*
	politeness	Ich **möchte** gerne mit Herrn Schmidt sprechen. *I'd like to speak to Herr Schmidt, please.*
müssen	obligation, instruction, necessity	Wir **müssen** das Exposé bis Montag abgeben. *We must deliver the exposé by Monday.* Sie **müssen** sich zuerst an der Pforte melden. *You'll have to check in at the front door.*

| sollen | indirect command, instruction | Herr Baumann hat gesagt, Sie **sollen** ihn zurückrufen. *Herr Baumann said you were to call him back.* |
| **wollen** | will, intention, aim | Wir **wollen** uns in diesem Marktsegment neu positionieren. *We want to establish a new position for ourselves in this market segment.* |

The word möchte is often used in spoken language. It's a form of the verb mögen and has no infinitive form of its own.

The present tense forms of the modal verbs:

	dürfen	**können**	**müssen**
ich	darf	kann	muss
du	darf-st	kann-st	muss-t
er/es/sie	darf	kann	muss
wir	dürf-en	könn-en	müss-en
ihr	dürf-t	könn-t	müss-t
sie/Sie	dürf-en	könn-en	müss-en

	wollen	**mögen**		**sollen**
ich	will	mag	möcht-e	soll
du	will-st	mag-st	möcht-e-st	soll-st
er/es/sie	will	mag	möcht-e	soll
wir	woll-en	mög-en	möcht-en	soll-en
ihr	woll-t	mög-t	möcht-et	soll-t
sie/Sie	woll-en	mög-en	möcht-en	soll-en

☼ Apart from möchte and sollen all the modal verbs change their main vowel in the singular.
The verb brauchen can be used with nur or nicht like a modal verb and then takes on the same meaning as müssen. The infinitive is then formed with zu.

Du **brauchst** mir das nicht auf**zu**schreiben, ich kann es mir so merken. *You don't have to write it down for me, I can remember it without.*
Du **musst** mir das nicht aufschreiben, ich kann es mir so merken. *You don't have to write it down for me, I can remember it without.*

Sometimes modal verbs can be used on their own without another main verb or infinitive:

Ich **will** ein Eis. *I want an ice cream.*
Sie **kann** das. *She can do it.*
Ihr **dürft** das. *You may (do that).*

Exercise 14
Please complete the following sentences with the appropriate modal verb.

a) .... Andrew Deutsch sprechen? – Ja, er
.... aber seine Kenntnisse noch erweitern.

b) .... du heute noch lernen? – Ja, ich
...........................!

c) Ich .... Ihnen doch bestimmt eine kleine
Erfrischung anbieten, oder …? – Ja, Sie
....

d) Bitte beachten Sie, dass Sie auf Bahnhöfen nicht rauchen ....

e) An dieser Stelle .... Sie nicht parken.

f) Du .... mit mir noch einige Worte sprechen?

g) Über das Jobsharing .... wir uns nochmals Gedanken machen.

h) Hier .... Sie leise sein.

7.3 Verben mit Präfix   Verbs with a Prefix
oder *Durchlesen und verstehen*

In German, lots of verbs can be combined with prefixes to form new verbs with different meanings.

If these prefixes are separable, then they also take the main stress when spoken.

• Separable prefixes are:

ab-	abholen	Peter **holt** Herrn Sailer vom Flughafen **ab.** *Peter is picking Herr Sailer up from the air-port.*
an-	anrufen	**Rufen** Sie mich nächste Woche wieder **an.** *Give me another call next week.*
auf-	aufmachen	Warten Sie, ich **mache** Ihnen die Tür **auf.** *Wait a moment, I'll open the door for you.*

aus-	ausfüllen	**Füllen** Sie bitte dieses Formular **aus**. *Please fill in this form.*
ein-	einstellen	Zum 1.10. **stellen** wir zehn neue Leute **ein**. *We shall be employing ten new people on 1st Oct.*
(he)raus- **(he)rein-**	heraus- kommen herein- kommen	**Kommen** Sie doch bitte **herein**! *Please do come in!*
her-	herstellen	Wir **stellen** optische Geräte **her**. *We manufacture optical equipment.*
hin-	hinfahren	In München ist eine Fach- tagung. Da **fahren** wir **hin**. *There's a conference in Munich. We're going there.*
mit-	mitbringen	Jeder **bringt** zur Bespre- chung neue Ideen **mit**. *Everyone will bring new ideas with them to the meeting.*
nach-	nachsehen	Ich **sehe** mal **nach**, ob Ihre Unterlagen schon fertig sind. *I'll just see if your documents are finished yet.*
vor-	vorstellen	Heute **stellen** sich die Bewerber für die Technikerstelle **vor**. *Today the applicants for the technician's job will be coming for an interview.*

weg-	weggehen	Herr Maier ist leider nicht da, er **geht** immer um vier Uhr **weg**. *Herr Maier isn't here unfortunately, he always leaves at four o'clock.*
weiter-	weiterleiten	Bitte **leiten** Sie diese Information an alle Abteilungsleiter **weiter**. *Please pass this information on to all heads of department.*
zu-	zuhören	Wir **hörten** alle gespannt **zu**. *We all listened attentively.*
zurück-	zurückkom-men	Frau Bolden **kommt** erst morgen früh von ihrer Dienstreise **zurück**. *Frau Bolden won't be back from her business trip until tomorrow morning.*

Prefixes that are inseparable are not stressed when spoken. As their name suggests, they cannot stand alone.

• Inseparable prefixes are:

be-	bearbeiten	Lydia **bearbeitet** die neue Produktbeschreibung. *Lydia is working on the description of the new product.*
emp-	empfehlen	Wir **empfehlen** die Vorteilspackung zu 1000 Stück. *We recommend the economy pack of 1000.*
ent-	entscheiden	Das **entscheidet** die Chefin. *The boss will decide that.*

er-	erschrecken	Diese Umsatzzahlen **erschrecken** die Aktionäre. *These sales figures will frighten the shareholders.*
ge-	gelingen	Die Überraschung ist dir wirklich **gelungen**. *You've succeeded in surprising us.*
miss-	missverstehen	Da haben Sie mich wohl **missverstanden**. *You must have misunderstood me.*
ver-	versuchen	Ich **versuche**, Frau Maiwald zu erreichen. *I'm trying to get hold of Frau Maiwald.*
zer-	zerbrechen	Die Vase ist **zerbrochen**. *The vase broke into pieces.*

Some prefixes can be either separable or inseparable. In each case the verb has a different meaning. These prefixes are durch-, über-, unter-, um-.

prefix	verb	separable, stressed	inseparable, unstressed
durch-	durchbrechen	Das dünne Eis bricht unter ihrem Gewicht durch. *The thin ice breaks under her weight.*	Die Globalisierungsgegner durchbrechen die Polizeiabsperrung. *The opponents of globalisation break through the police barrier.*
über-	übersetzen	Wir setzen von Calais nach Dover über. *We're taking the ferry from Calais to Dover.*	Bitte übersetzen Sie diesen Text. *Please translate this text.*

prefix	verb	separable, stressed	inseparable, unstressed
unter-	untergehen	Es ist schon spät, die Sonne **geht** schon **unter**. *It's late, the sun is already setting.*	
	unterbrechen		Niemand **unterbrach** den Redner. *No one interrupted the speaker.*
um-	umstellen	Wir **stellen** unser Produktsortiment völlig **um**. *We are changing our range of products completely.*	Der Bankräuber konnte nicht mehr fliehen – das Gebäude war **umstellt**. *The bankrobber couldn't escape – the building was surrounded.*

Exercise 15

Please fill in the correct separable and inseparable verbs.

a) verfallen: Durch die Euro-Einführung ....

   bestimmte Briefmarken.

b) anfangen: Der Film „Harry Potter" ....

   um 20:00 Uhr ....

c) übersetzen: Herr Brown .... den Text

   ins Deutsche ....

d) umschreiben: Der Lehrer .... die

   unbekannte Vokabel mit Synonymen ....

e) abgeben: Der Kurier .... das Paket an

der Pforte ....

f) umziehen: Am Sonntag .... Pamela in

die neue Wohnung ....

g) gefallen: Der Dom und die Steinerne Brücke in

Regensburg .... mir ....

h) ausfallen: Das Training-on-the-Job ....

heute ....

i) unterstellen: Dieses böswillige Verhalten

.... man Kim ....

j) zerfallen: Die Tagesordnung .... in acht

umfangreiche Punkte ....

7.4 Verben mit festen Präpositionen
Verbs with Fixed Prepositions
oder *Sich auf etwas freuen*

In German, similar to English, there are lots of verbs that form a close relationship with certain prepositions. These prepositional verbs then take on another meaning. The preposition defines the case of the noun that follows.

• sich freuen über + accusative

Isabelle hat eine sehr gute Note in der Prüfung bekommen. *Isabelle got good marks in the exam.*
Sie **freut sich über** das Ergebnis. *She is very pleased about the result.*

- sich freuen auf + accusative

Isabelle freut sich auf ihr Praktikum nächsten Monat.
Isabelle is looking forward to her work programme next month.

- einladen zu + dative

Wir laden Sie zur Einweihung unserer neuen Firmenräume ein. *We'd like to invite you to the official opening of our new offices.*

- sich entschuldigen bei + dative,
  sich entschuldigen für + accusative

Herr Maiwald hat sich bei uns für die verspätete Lieferung entschuldigt. *Herr Maiwald apologized to us for the late delivery.*

L! Always try to think of these prepositional verbs as single expressions and learn them as one item, e. g.: denken an + accusative. In the appendix (▸ p. 175 ff.) you'll find a list of the most important ones.

8 Präsens und Imperativ
Present Tense and Imperative
oder *Jetzt und sofort*

Haben Sie Blumen, die „Alles Gute zum Hochzeits-tag" sagen?

Lasst Blumen sprechen

Say it with flowers. – Have you got flowers that say "Happy anniversary?"

The present tense in German is more than just a way of expressing present time. It can be used almost universally. But first let's look at the various forms of the verb in the present tense.

8.1 Formen des Präsens
Forms of Present Tense
oder *Regelmäßig und unregelmäßig*

To form the present tense correctly you have to remember two things:

• Firstly, the correct ending: formed by removing the -en from the end of the infinitive and replacing it with the ending appropriate to the person (▶ ❼, p. 75).

- Secondly, you have to know whether you are dealing with a regular (or weak) verb – in which case the verb stem remains the same for all persons. Irregular verbs (also called strong verbs), on the other hand, undergo a vowel change in the main stem and sometimes change the stem completely. Fortunately this happens only in the 2nd and 3rd person singular.

	wohnen to live (regular)	arbeiten to work (regular)	fahren to go/to drive (irregular)	nehmen to take (irregular)
ich	wohn-**e**	arbeit-**e**	fahr-**e**	nehm-**e**
du	wohn-**st**	arbeit-**est**	fähr-**st**	nimm-**st**
er/es/sie	wohn-**t**	arbeit-**et**	fähr-**t**	nimm-**t**
wir	wohn-**en**	arbeit-**en**	fahr-**en**	nehm-**en**
ihr	wohn-**t**	arbeit-**et**	fahr-**t**	nehm-**t**
sie/Sie	wohn-**en**	arbeit-**en**	fahr-**en**	nehm-**en**

The present tense forms of the auxiliary and modal verbs can be found in **7.1** and **7.2** (▷ p. 75 ff.).

⚡ Verbs whose stem ends in **-t** or **-d** add an **-e-** before the endings **-st** or **-t** to make pronunciation easier:

reden *to speak;* **arbeiten** *to work:*
du red**e**st, er red**e**t; *you speak, he speaks;*
ihr arbeit**e**t *you work (plural)*

☼ Infinitives, the 1st and 3rd person plural have the same form: **wohnen**: wir wohn**en**, sie/Sie wohn**en**.

Whether a verb is regular or irregular has to be learnt by heart. In the appendix (▷ p. 165 ff.) you'll find a list of the most important irregular verbs.

8.2 Gebrauch des Präsens   Use of Present Tense
oder *Heute, morgen, immer*

The present tense can be used in so many different ways that we could almost regard it as a kind of universal tool. Its main function is to describe something happening in the present. But it can also convey a large number of other meanings:

something happening now	Anna **hält** eine Rede. *Anna is making a speech.*
something that happens regularly	Wir **treffen** uns montags um 10 Uhr zur Teambesprechung. *We meet every Monday at 10 for a team talk.*
a general rule	Die Sonne **geht** im Osten **auf**. *The sun rises in the east.*
something started in the past and is still going on	Wir **sind** seit 10 Jahren verheiratet. *We have been married for 10 years.*
something happening in the future	Nächste Woche **kommt** die neue Personalchefin. *The new head of personnel is coming next week.*
a story from the past told vividly	Da waren wir also in Rom. Und wie ich so im Café **sitze**, da **kommt** Frau Smith von unserer Tochtergesellschaft in Los Angeles, und sie **sagt**: … *We were in Rome. And just as I'm sitting there in the café, in comes Frau Smith from our Los Angeles branch and she says to me: …*

⚡ If the present tense is used to describe a future event, then an expression of time (adverb or adverbial phrase) should be used to make things clear: nächste Woche, morgen, nächsten Montag … *(next week, tomorrow, next Monday …).*

8.3 Imperativ Imperative
oder *Sei still!*

The imperative is used for orders, instructions, requests and advice made or given to another person directly. The imperative has the following forms:

	singular	plural
	address: du	*address:* ihr
informal (no pronoun)	**Nimm** doch Platz! *Take a seat.*	**Nehmt** doch Platz! *Take a seat.*
	Fahr vorsichtig! *Drive carefully.*	**Fahrt** vorsichtig! *Drive carefully.*
	Sei still! *Be quiet.*	**Seid** still! *Be quiet.*
formal (pronoun obligatory)	**Nehmen Sie** doch Platz! *Take a seat.*	**Nehmen Sie** doch Platz! *Take a seat.*
	Fahren Sie vorsichtig! *Drive carefully.*	**Fahren Sie** vorsichtig! *Drive carefully.*
	Seien Sie still! *Be quiet.*	**Seien Sie** still! *Be quiet.*

• Informal imperative
The informal imperative singular is formed from the 2nd person singular of the present tense without -st; in the plural it is identical to the 2nd person plural:

du nimmst, imperative: **nimm!** *take*
ihr nehmt, imperative: **nehmt!** *take*

• Formal imperative

Here the imperative is identical to the 3rd person plural present tense. The pronoun takes second place.

Sie nehmen, imperative: **Nehmen Sie!** *take*

In a sentence the imperative comes first (▷ ⑥, p. 67 ff.). With separable verbs the inflected part comes first and the separable part at the end of the sentence. A sentence can, however, also start with bitte or the name of the person addressed.

order	Felix, **sitz**! *Felix, sit!*
instruction	**Schneiden Sie** das Gemüse in dünne Scheiben. *Cut the vegetables into thin slices.*
request	Frau Schweizer, **bringen Sie** mir bitte das Angebot der Firma Etech. *Frau Schweitzer, bring me that offer from Etech, would you, please?*
	Bitte **melden Sie** uns zu dieser Konferenz **an**! *Please let them know we wish to attend the conference.*
advice	**Probier** doch mal die Atemübungen zur Stressbewältigung **aus**. *Try breathing exercises to relieve stress.*

⚡ A bare imperative is very direct and can often sound curt, if not a little rude. It becomes much more polite through the use of bitte *please,* suitable modal particles and, of course, friendly intonation or even smiling.

Verbinden Sie mich **bitte** mit Herrn Gässlein! *Please put me through to Herr Gässlein!*
Halt **doch bitte** hier **mal** an! *Stop here, please, will you?*

Exercise 16

Please put the following sentences into the imperative using the word bitte.

a) Sie sollten sich um den Job als Trainee bewerben.

....

b) Du solltest an dem Kurs in der Sprachenschule teilnehmen.

....

c) Sie sollten nicht im Gang rauchen.

....

d) Du solltest fragen, wenn dir eine Redewendung nicht bekannt ist.

....

e) Ihr solltet pünktlich kommen.

....

9 Vergangenheit Past Tenses
oder *Lang ist's her*

Was hast du für schöne Blumen mitgebracht! Die gleichen habe ich im Garten.

Hattest du, Tante Ilse, hattest du.

What nice flowers you've brought me! I have the same ones in the garden. – You had, aunt Ilse, you had.

Here's a short explanation of the relevant past tense forms. But be careful: some of the terms used correspond with their English equivalent and some don't.

To talk about the past in German we almost always use the *Perfekt* or perfect tense. Sometimes this is used in exactly the same way as in English (i.e. the present perfect) but more often than not it is used in the same way as the English simple past. This is an important contrast that you need to remember.

Peter: Und, wie **hat** dir der Film **gefallen**?
Peter: Well, how did you like the film?

When using auxiliary and modal verbs and in more formal situations, however, the *Präteritum* is preferred. This is also true in written language.

Alan: Echt super, **war** total spannend.
        Super film, it was really exciting.
Peter: Ich **wollte** es eigentlich im Urlaub **lesen** …
        I was going to read it while I'm on holiday.
Zeitungsmeldung: *newspaper article:*
Auf der eisglatten Straße **kam** das Fahrzeug ins
Schleudern und **geriet** auf die andere Fahrbahn.
*On the icy road the car skidded and swerved into
oncoming traffic.*

To complete the spectrum of past tense forms the third
tense we need to talk about is the *Plusquamperfekt* or
past perfect tense.

9.1   Präteritum   **Past Simple**
oder *Es war einmal*

The Präteritum or past simple in German is formed differ-
ently depending on whether the verb is regular and weak
or irregular and strong.

• Irregular verbs Starke Verben

These verbs change the vowel in their main stem. They
have normal personal endings:

geben   Präteritum/past simple: Früher **gab** es viele
                                     Dinosaurier. *In earlier
                                     times there were lots of
                                     dinosaurs.*
gehen   Präteritum/past simple: Wir **gingen** ins Kino.
                                     We went to the cinema.
                                     stem + ending

• Regular verbs Schwache Verben

Regular verbs do not change the vowel in their main stem. The past simple tense is indicated instead by the addition of -(e)te- after the main stem:

leben	Präteritum/past simple:	Die Dinosaurier lebten vor Millionen von Jahren. *The dinosaurs lived millions of years ago.* stem + **-te-** + ending

In the past simple both weak and strong verbs take the normal endings in all persons, which means no endings in the 1st and 3rd person singular and endings in the plural and in the 2nd person singular (▶ ⑦, p. 75).

The following table will help you to remember:

	leben (weak)	antworten (weak)	geben (strong)	rufen (strong)
ich	leb-**te**	antwort-**ete**	gab	rief
du	leb-**te**-st	antwort-**ete**-st	gab-**st**	rief-**st**
er/es/sie	leb-**te**	antwort-**ete**	gab	rief
wir	leb-**te**-n	antwort-**ete**-n	gab-**en**	rief-**en**
ihr	leb-**te**-t	antwort-**ete**-t	gab-**t**	rief-**t**
sie/Sie	leb-**te**-n	antwort-**ete**-n	gab-**en**	rief-**en**

➕ Verbs whose stem ends in -d, -t, -m or -n, indicate the Präteritum/past simple by adding -ete-.

• Mixed verbs Mischverben

Some verbs change their main vowel like a strong verb but still take the weak verb ending -(e)te- for the Präteritum:

brennen Präteritum/past simple: Die Lagerhallen brannten. *The ware-houses were burning.* stem + **-te-** + ending

Here you can see that the past simple can also express the continuous or progressive form that you know from English.

There's no easy way around it unfortunately: You have to learn the strong and mixed verbs and their forms by heart. ▷ page 165 ff. to help you.

• Modal verbs Modalverben

Modal verbs form the past simple in the same way as weak verbs, but they lose their Umlaut in the process.

	durf	konn	muss	woll	moch	soll
ich	-te	-te	-te	-te	-te	-te
du	-te-st	-te-st	-te-st	-te-st	-te-st	-te-st
er/es/sie	-te	-te	-te	-te	-te	-te
wir	-te-n	-te-n	-te-n	-te-n	-te-n	-te-n
ihr	-te-t	-te-t	-te-t	-te-t	-te-t	-te-t
sie/Sie	-te-n	-te-n	-te-n	-te-n	-te-n	-te-n

Auxiliary verbs have quite different forms in the past simple:

	sein	**haben**	**werden**
ich	war	hat-**te**	wur-**de**
du	war-**st**	hat-**te-st**	wur-**de-st**
er/es/sie	war	hat-**te**	wur-**de**
wir	war-**en**	hat-**te-n**	wur-**de-n**
ihr	war-**t**	hat-**te-t**	wur-**de-t**
sie/Sie	war-**en**	hat-**te-n**	wur-**de-n**

9.2 Partizip II   Past Participle
oder *Gelernt ist gelernt*

We need the past (or: perfect) participle *Partizip II* to form the present perfect, but it is also used in the past perfect.

• Present Perfect Perfekt

Igor hat Elena eine E-Mail **geschrieben**. (← schreiben)
Igor has written/wrote Elena an e-mail.
Elena hat zuerst nicht **gewusst**, ob sie zurückschreiben soll. (← wissen)
Elena didn't know at first whether she should reply.
Aber dann hat Elena doch **geantwortet**. (← antworten)
But then Elena did answer after all.

• Past Perfect Plusquamperfekt

Weil er die Unterlagen **vergessen** hatte, musste er zurück ins Büro.
Because he had forgotten the papers, he had to go back to the office.

There are numerous ways to form the past participle. Here is a short summary followed by a more detailed explanation.

infinitive	past participle				
	prefix	ge-	stem	ending	
studieren	–	–	studier-	-t	*study*
kaufen	–	ge-	-kauf-	-t	*buy*
einkaufen	ein-	-ge-	-kauf-	-t	*do some shopping*
verkaufen	ver-	–	-kauf-	-t	*sell*
sprechen	–	ge-	-sproch-	-en	*speak*
ansprechen	an-	-ge-	-sproch-	-en	*speak to s. o.*
versprechen	ver-	–	-sproch-	-en	*promise*
denken	–	ge-	-dach-	-t	*think*

The easiest verbs to deal with are those ending in -ieren:

infinitive		past participle	
studieren	→	studiert	*study*
demonstrieren	→	demonstriert	*demonstrate*
fotokopieren	→	fotokopiert	*photocopy*

To form the past participle we simply replace the infinitive ending -en with -t. It may encourage you to know that the number of verbs in this group is constantly increasing due to the adoption into German of new words from other languages.

With all other verbs the matter is more complicated. Try to imagine verbs as the population of a country. There you have average citizens – these are our weak or regular verbs and they form the largest section of the population.

The past participle of these verbs has two identification marks: the prefix ge- and the participle ending -(e)t which replaces the infinitive ending -en. The main part of the verb remains unchanged.

infinitive		past participle	
kaufen	→	gekauft	*buy – bought*
arbeiten	→	gearbeitet	*work – worked*
spielen	→	gespielt	*play – played*

Of course, even average citizens are not all the same and weak verbs can be divided into:

• Simple verbs

kaufen	gekauft	ge- at the beginning	*buy – bought*

• Verbs with separable prefix

einkaufen	eingekauft	ge- between prefix and main stem	*buy – bought*

• Verbs with inseparable prefix

verkaufen	verkauft	no ge-	*sell – sold*

Every country has its average citizens, but it also has people who don't conform. You might call them revolutionaries or rebels who are just different. These would be our strong or irregular verbs (starke/unregelmäßige Verben).

They take on only the ge- as identification. The ending -en remains the same as in the infinitive. Many of them do, however, change the main stem.

infinitive		past participle	
sprechen	→	**ge**sprochen	*speak – spoken*
kommen	→	**ge**kommen	*come – come*
nehmen	→	**ge**nommen	*take – taken*

Our rebels, too, can be divided into:

• Simple verbs

sprechen	→ **ge-** sprochen	**ge-** at the beginning	*speak – spoken*

• Verbs with separable prefix

an- sprechen	→ an**ge-** sprochen	**ge-** between pre- fix and main stem	*speak to – spoken to*

• Verbs with inseparable prefix

ver- sprechen	→ ver- sprochen	no **ge-**	*promise – promised*

Rebel groups often cause problems. It's no different with German verbs.

Next we have a group we might call the "spies" or "undercover agents". They are the smallest group of all and they look a bit like ordinary citizens but with a few rebel elements thrown in. These are the so-called mixed verbs gemischte Verben. They change their stem, but have both ge- and the ending -(e)t in the past participle nevertheless.

infinitive	past participle	
denken	gedacht	*think – thought*
bringen	gebracht	*bring – brought*
rennen	gerannt	*run – run*

L! You have to learn the irregular and mixed verbs by heart. It's easiest if you learn them in groups according to the way they change their main vowel. There are three possibilities:

A – B – A:	schlafen	–	schlief	–	geschlafen
A – B – B:	fliegen	–	flog	–	geflogen
A – B – C:	sprechen	–	sprach	–	gesprochen

▷ In the appendix you'll find a list of the most important irregular and mixed verbs. To finish off this section here is a short survey:

verb type	infinitive	past participle	prefix	ge-	stem can change	ending
-ieren	studieren	studiert	no	no	no	-(e)t
simple verbs	kaufen	gekauft	no	yes	no	-(e)t
	sprechen	gesprochen	no	yes	yes	-(e)n
	denken	gedacht	no	yes	yes	-(e)t
verbs with separable prefix	einkaufen	eingekauft	yes	yes	no	-(e)t
	an- sprechen	ange- sprochen	yes	yes	yes	-(e)n
verbs with inseparable prefix	verkaufen	verkauft	yes	no	no	-(e)t
	versprechen	versprochen	yes	no	yes	-(e)n

9.3 Perfekt Present Perfect
oder *Sein oder haben?*

The present perfect is formed using the present tense of either sein or haben together with the past participle.

> Wir **sind** gestern ins Kino **gegangen** und **haben** einen schönen Film **gesehen.** *We went to the cinema yesterday and saw a great film.*

But when do we use sein and when do we use haben?

• The Present Perfect with sein

Sein is used to form the present perfect in only very few cases. It's easiest, therefore, if you just learn this small group and then use haben for all the rest.

We use sein in the present perfect of the following verbs:

sein	**ist** gewesen	*be – has been/was*
bleiben	**ist** geblieben	*stay – has stayed/stayed*
werden	**ist** geworden	*become – has become/became*

passieren, geschehen and verbs with similar meaning:

passieren	ist passiert	*happen –*
		has happened/happened
geschehen	ist geschehen	*happen –*
		has happened/happened

Verbs indicating movement from A to B:

Herr Schneider **ist** zur Messe nach Leipzig **gefahren**.
Herr Schneider has gone to the fair in Leipzig.
Maria **ist** kurz in den Keller **gegangen**. *Maria has just gone down to the cellar.*

Verbs indicating a change of state:

Jan **ist** während des Vortrags von Herrn Verhusen **eingeschlafen**. *Jan fell asleep during Herr Verhusen's talk.*
Kind, du **bist** aber **gewachsen**! *How you've grown, child!*

• The Present Perfect with haben

Most verbs form the present perfect tense with haben, especially reflexive verbs, verbs that take an accusative object and modal verbs.

Reflexive verbs:
Herr Niemer **hat sich** gut auf die Besprechung **vorbereitet**. *Herr Niemer has prepared well for the meeting.*
Verbs with an accusative object:
Nina **hat** ihr Motorrad in die Garage **gefahren**. *Nina has driven her motorbike into the garage.*
Modal verbs:
Das tut mir leid, ich **habe** das nicht **gewollt**. *I'm sorry, I didn't want that to happen.*

Modal verbs are not very often used in the present perfect. Normally they are used in the past simple.

⚡ Verbs that, due to the addition of a prefix, take on a different meaning may need either sein or haben.

Er **ist** den New-York-Marathon gelaufen. *He ran the New York Marathon.*
Die Kosten **haben** sich auf 100 Euro belaufen. *The expenses summed up to 100 euros.*

9.4   Plusquamperfekt   Past Perfect
oder *Ich hatte vergessen …*

The past perfect indicates a time before the normal past. It is used to describe an event that happened before another event in the past.

Als wir in Paris ankamen, **hatten** unsere Geschäftspartner bereits alles für die Konferenz **vorbereitet**. *When we arrived in Paris, our business partners had already prepared everything for the conference.*

Bevor wir weggefahren sind, **hatte** ich alle Pflanzen **gegossen**. *Before we left, I had watered all the plants.*

Nachdem Frau Malina die neuen Teammitglieder **begrüßt hatte**, arbeiteten wir konsequent die Tagesordnung durch. *After Frau Malina had greeted the new team members, we went through the agenda thoroughly.*

Forming the past perfect is very easy. It's done in exactly the same way as the present perfect, but instead of using the present tense of sein or haben, we use the past simple.

present perfect	past perfect
Wir **haben** die Verträge abgeschlossen. *We have concluded the contracts.*	Wir **hatten** die Verträge abgeschlossen. *We had concluded the contracts.*
Ihr **seid** zur Besprechung gekommen. *You have come to the meeting.*	Ihr **wart** zur Besprechung gekommen. *You had come to the meeting.*

Here is a short survey of the forms of the past perfect:

	sagen *to say*		**kommen** *to come*	
ich	hatte	gesagt	war	gekommen
du	hattest	gesagt	warst	gekommen
er/es/sie	hatte	gesagt	war	gekommen
wir	hatten	gesagt	waren	gekommen
ihr	hattet	gesagt	wart	gekommen
sie/Sie	hatten	gesagt	waren	gekommen

Exercise 17

Please put the following sentences into the Präteritum and Perfekt.

a) Herr White bucht für Donnerstag einen Flug nach Deutschland.

b) Er kommt am Flughafen Berlin-Tegel an und steigt in das nächste Taxi.

c) Dieses fährt Herrn White in das Hotel „Zum Goldenen Stern".

d) An der Rezeption erhält er die Schlüssel für sein Zimmer.

e) Um 15:00 Uhr trifft sich Herr White mit seinen Geschäftspartnern.

f) Diese erklären ihm die neue geschäftliche Situation und bitten um Verständnis.

g) Herr White unterbricht die Verhandlungen und zieht einen neuen Termin in Betracht.

h) Am nächsten Morgen holt Herr White seine Frau vom Flughafen ab.

i) Gemeinsam verbringen sie einige Tage in Berlin.

j) Frau und Herr White sehen sich noch am selben Tag das Brandenburger Tor an.

k) Am folgenden Tag besichtigen sie den Reichstag.

l) Am letzten Tag ihres Urlaubs fahren sie auf den Fernsehturm und werfen einen Blick auf die Dächer Berlins.

Exercise 18

Please put the parts in bold print into the Plusquam-perfekt.

a) Nachdem wir einen Nachsendeauftrag bei der Post stellten, fuhren wir in den Urlaub.

b) Nachdem Eileen die Führerscheinprüfung bestand, feierten wir das erfreuliche Ereignis mit einem Gläschen Sekt.

c) Nachdem Marcus die Vor- und Nachteile darstellte, gingen wir zur Aussprache über.

d) Nachdem der Chef von seiner Auslandsreise zurückkam, wurde das umstrittene Projekt nochmals besprochen.

e) Nachdem die Abteilungsleiter eintrafen, diskutierten wir über das weitere Vorgehen.

10 **Futur** **Future Tense**
oder *Was sein wird*

Wir werden in wenigen Minuten in Frankfurt landen.

We´ll be landing at Frankfort in a few minutes.

Although you can quite easily use the present tense to talk about the future (▷ ⑧, p. 89 ff.), there are also special future tense forms.

10.1 **Futur I** **Future Tense**
oder *Sie werden es schaffen*

We use the future tense to talk about an event in the future or to express what we expect or assume will take place.

• Event in the future

Wir **werden** (im Sommer) nach Gran Canaria **fliegen.**
We are going to fly to Gran Canaria in the summer.

• Expectation

Hans wird dir sicherlich ein Souvenir **mitbringen.**
Hans will certainly bring you back a souvenir.

• Assumption

Bei dem Schneetreiben **werden** sich die Gäste
wahrscheinlich **verspäten.** *In this snowstorm the guests
will probably be late.*
Wir **werden** im Sommer vielleicht nach Gran Canaria
fliegen. *Perhaps we'll fly to Gran Canaria in the summer.*

The future tense is formed with the present tense of the
verb werden plus the infinitive.

	werden +	infinitive
ich	werde	feiern
du	wirst	feiern
er/es/sie	wird	feiern
wir	werden	feiern
ihr	werdet	feiern
sie/Sie	werden	feiern

⚡ In any one sentence you use werden only once:

Mach dir keine Sorgen. Das **wird** schon gut (werden).
Don't worry. It'll be OK.

10.2 Futur II Future Perfect
oder *Sie werden es geschafft haben*

The future perfect is used far less frequently than the future. But you ought to be able to recognise and understand it when it occurs. We use the future perfect to talk about an event that will be completed in the future.

In zwei Jahren **wirst** du dein Studium **abgeschlossen haben.** *In two years you will have finished your studies.* Nächsten Freitag um diese Uhrzeit **werden** wir die Präsentation bereits hinter uns **gebracht haben.** *By this time next Friday we will have already done the presentation.*

We can also use the future perfect to express an assumption about a past event.

Herr Miller **wird** uns **geschrieben haben,** als wir im Urlaub waren. *Herr Miller will haven written to us while we were on holiday.*

The future perfect is formed using the present tense of the verb werden plus the past participle plus haben or sein.

Ende des Jahres **werden** wir **gefeiert haben** und viele Gäste **werden gekommen sein.** *At the end of the year we will have had our party and lots of guests will have come.*
Im nächsten Sommer **werden** wir die Filiale **eröffnet haben** und die Presse **wird** dabei **gewesen sein.** *Next summer we will have opened our new branch and the press will have been there.*

☀ We often use the present perfect in German instead of the future perfect.

> In zwei Jahren **hast** du dein Studium **abgeschlossen.**
> *In two years you will have finished your studies.*
> Nächsten Freitag um diese Uhrzeit **haben** wir die
> Präsentation bereits hinter uns **gebracht.** *By this time*
> *next Friday we will have already done the presentation.*

Exercise 19
Please put all the sentences in exercise 17 into the future tense.

a) ....

b) ....

c) ....

d) ....

e) ....

f) ....

g) ....

h) ....

i) ....

j) ....

k) ....

l) ....

11 Konjunktiv Subjunctive
oder *Wünsche und indirekte Rede*

Ich würde gerne das Kleid im Schaufenster anprobieren.

Wie Sie wünschen. Wir haben aber auch Umkleidekabinen.

I would like to try the dress in the shop window. – As you wish, Madam, but we also have fitting rooms.

11.1 Konjunktiv I Present Subjunctive
oder *Er sagte, dass er komme*

The present subjunctive occurs nearly always in written language only and is used exclusively to express indirect or reported speech *indirekte Rede*. Colloquially, indirect speech is usually expressed using the same forms of the verb as in direct speech *direkte Rede*.

Direct speech:

Michael: „Ich **kann** am Samstag leider nicht zur Party **kommen**."

Michael: "I can't come to the party on Saturday, unfortunately."

Reported speech (colloquial):

Anke: „Michael sagte, dass er am Samstag nicht zur Party **kommen kann**."

Anke: "Michael said that he couldn't come to the party on Saturday."

Reported speech (formal) with present subjunctive:

Anke: „Michael sagte, dass er am Samstag nicht zur Party **kommen könne**."

Anke: "Michael said that he couldn't come to the party on Saturday."

The present subjunctive is formed as follows:
Main stem of the infinitive without an ending + -e- + normal ending for the appropriate person. (▷ **7**, p. 75)
A double -e disappears.

present subjunctive	
ich	hab-e
du	hab-e-st
er/es/sie	hab-e
wir	hab-e-n
ihr	hab-e-t
sie/Sie	hab-e-n

The forms of the present subjunctive are sometimes identical to those of the present indicative. When this happens in reported speech, we fall back on the past subjunctive *Konjunktiv II* or würde + **infinitive** (▶ **11.2** , p. 117).

Direct speech:
Mona: „Unsere koreanischen Partner **bleiben** eine Woche."
Mona: "Our Korean partners are staying for a week."
Reported speech with present subjunctive:
Jan: „Mona sagt, unsere koreanischen Partner **bleiben** eine Woche."
Jan: "Mona says our Korean partners are staying for a week."
Reported speech with past subjunctive:
Jan: „Mona sagte, unsere koreanischen Partner **würden** eine Woche **bleiben**."
Jan: "Mona said our Korean partners were staying for a week."

The verb sein *to be* is once again a special case.

present subjunctive	
ich	sei
du	seist
er/es/sie	sei
wir	seien
ihr	sei(e)t
sie/Sie	seien

⚡ The present subjunctive is most frequently used in the 3rd person singular:

er/es/sie **habe**
er/es/sie **werde**
er/es/sie **müsse**
er/es/sie **wolle**
er/es/sie **könne**
er/es/sie **kaufe**
...

What else do we need to know about reported speech? It is introduced by a main clause containing a verb of "saying" or "reporting".

Der Pressesprecher **sagte,** dass es sich dabei nur um ein Gerücht **handle.** *The press spokesman said that it was only a rumour.*
Martina **sagt,** Ulrike **sei** krank. *Martina says Ulrike is ill.*

The personal pronouns may change.

direct speech	reported speech
Bozena: „**Ich** nehme ein Taxi." *Bozena: "I'll take a taxi."*	Martha: „Bozena sagt, **sie** nehme ein Taxi." *Martha: "Bozena says she'll take a taxi."*
Die Teammitglieder: „**Wir** brauchen mehr Zeit." *The team: "We need more time."*	Die Chefsekretärin: „Die Teammitglieder sagen, **sie** brauchen mehr Zeit." *The boss's secretary: "The team say they need more time."*

11.2 Konjunktiv II Past Subjunctive
oder *Hätte ich, dann würde ich*

The past subjunctive serves either as a substitute for the present subjunctive (▷ **11.1**, p. 114), or it is used to express an unreal condition, a presumption, speculation, a polite wish or request.

Substitute for the present subjunctive:
Mira sagt, die Jungs **hätten** zu viel **getrunken**. *Mira says the boys drank too much.*
An unreal condition:
Wenn ich reich wäre, **würde** ich den Winter immer im Süden **verbringen**. *If I were rich, I'd always spend the winter down south.*
Presumption/speculation:
Es **könnte** ja auch sein, dass Hans noch im Stau steht. *It could well be that Hans is still caught up in a traffic jam.*
Polite wish or request:
Herr Bisowski, **könnten** Sie mir bitte die Unterlagen der Firma Fallmer bringen? *Herr Bisowski, could you bring me the Fallmer documents, please?*

The past subjunctive is formed in two different ways:

• With weak verbs the past subjunctive and the past simple are identical:

past simple: ich reiste …
past subjunctive: ich reiste …

To avoid confusion a substitute form is used:
würde (= past subjunctive of werden) + infinitive

ich **würde reisen** *I travelled/I would travel*
du **würdest kochen** *you cooked/you would cook*

• With strong verbs, on the other hand, the past simple
forms the base: The signal ending -e is added together
with an Umlaut on the main vowel.

ich käm**e** (← kommen; past simple: ich kam)
I came/I would come
er träf**e** (← treffen; past simple: er traf)
he met/he would meet
sie schrieb**e** (← schreiben; past simple: sie schrieb)
she wrote/she would write

Nevertheless, even with strong verbs, especially in everyday speech, we use würde + infinitive. It is the most
common form of the past subjunctive in German.

	werden +	**infinitive**
ich	würde	fragen
du	würdest	fragen
er/es/sie	würde	fragen
wir	würden	fragen
ihr	würdet	fragen
sie/Sie	würden	fragen

It's only in the case of auxiliary and modal verbs that we
find independent forms of the past subjunctive in common use.

past subjunctive							
	sein	**haben**	**dürfen**	**können**	**müssen**	**wollen**	**sollen**
ich	wär	hätt	dürft	könnt	müsst	wollt	sollt
	-e	-e	-e	-e	-e	-e	-e
du	wär	hätt	dürft	könnt	müsst	wollt	sollt
	-(e)st	-est	-est	-est	-est	-est	-est
er/es/sie	wär	hätt	dürft	könnt	müsst	wollt	sollt
	-e	-e	-e	-e	-e	-e	-e
wir	wär	hätt	dürft	könnt	müsst	wollt	sollt
	-en	-en	-en	-en	-en	-en	-en
ihr	wär	hätt	dürft	könnt	müsst	wollt	sollt
	-(e)t	-et	-et	-et	-et	-et	-et
sie/Sie	wär	hätt	dürft	könnt	müsst	wollt	sollt
	-en	-en	-en	-en	-en	-en	-en

The past perfect subjunctive is formed using the past subjunctive of sein or haben + the past participle.

Wir **wären** ja gerne zum Frühlingsfest **gekommen**, aber wir waren leider verhindert. *We would have liked to come to the spring party, but unfortunately something came up.*
Wenn die Besprechung gestern Abend nicht so lange **gedauert hätte, wäre** ich sicher noch zum Training **gekommen**. *If the meeting yesterday evening hadn't lasted so long, I would have made it to the training for sure.*

Exercise 20
Please change the direct speech in the following sentences into reported speech.

a) Herr Miller sagt: „Ich bin mit meiner neuen Marketingassistentin sehr zufrieden."

b) Frau Dinz erläutert: „Durch das neue Computerprogramm können wir die Absatzzahlen schneller ermitteln."

c) Der Verkäufer erklärt: „Das neue Handy verfügt über eine USB-Schnittstelle."

d) Die Angestellte erwidert: „Durch mehr Personal erreichen wir eine bessere Kundenbindung."

e) Der Chef sagt: „Ich bin mit der Arbeitsweise von Frau Gordon sehr zufrieden."

Exercise 21
Please complete the following sentences with the correct form of the verb in the past subjunctive.

a) .... ich Sie kurz stören? (dürfen)

b) .... du das für mich kopieren? (können)

c) Das .... wirklich nett von dir. (sein)

d) Wenn ich eine eigene Firma ...., dann

.... ich mit den Mitarbeitern jeden

Morgen Tai-Chi .... (haben/machen)

e) So eine Katastrophe! Das alles .... nicht

..........................., wenn ich besser ....

.... (passieren/aufpassen)!

12 Passiv Passive
oder *Das muss gemacht werden*

Meine Damen, ich möchte Ihnen mal zeigen, was anderswo geleistet wird.

Ladies, I'd like to show you what's being accomplished elsewhere.

In the passive form of the verb it's not the person that's important but what happens. The passive is used to express what happens to a thing or person, not what a thing or person does. The actual doer is irrelevant, not identifiable or needs to remain unknown.

Das Regal **wird zusammengebaut**. *The shelves are being put together.*
Die Seitenteile **werden** an der Bodenplatte **festgemacht**. *The side pieces get fixed to the base.*
Der Auftrag **ist vergeben worden**. *The job has been assigned.*

The passive tends to be used most in academic texts, lists of instructions etc. There are two forms: the passive describing an action and the passive describing a state.

12.1 Vorgangspassiv Passive Expressing Action
oder *Das Regal wird aufgebaut*

As in English, verbs with an accusative object almost always have a passive form. The accusative object in the active sentence becomes the subject of the passive sentence. If we still need to name the person involved, we add the preposition von.

active: **Dr. Kappler untersucht den Jungen.**
subject   accusative object
Dr Kappler is examining the boy.
passive: **Der Junge wird (von Dr. Kappler) untersucht.**
subject + auxiliary verb + (**von** + agent) past
                    werden   participle
The boy is being examined (by Dr Kappler).

Sometimes von is replaced by durch.

Die Häuser **wurden** (durch das Erdbeben) schwer **beschädigt**.
subject + auxiliary verb + (durch + agent) past participle
                    werden
The houses were badly damaged (by the earthquake).

Just like the active, the passive occurs in all tenses and also in the subjunctive. Formation follows the same system as the active, always using a form of the verb werden. Here is a list of all the passive forms in the various tenses:

- Present Tense

	present tense of werden	+ past participle	
ich	werde	geliebt	*(Someone) loves me.*
du	wirst	angerufen	*There's a telephone call for you.*
er/es/sie	wird	gefüttert	*He/It/She is being fed.*
wir	werden	benachrichtigt	*We're getting the news.*
ihr	werdet	überrascht	*You'll be surprised.*
sie/Sie	werden	abgeholt	*They/You are getting picked up.*

As you can see from the English translation of the example sentences, the passive is often used in German to express a certain idea, whereas it would not be natural to use the passive in other languages and the other way round (▷ **12.2** , p. 128 man)! This is especially true for present tense forms. It is best, of course, to learn these in context since the choice of an active or passive construction always depends on the meaning of the individual verb and the intention of the speaker.

- Past Simple

	past simple of + past participle werden		
ich	wurde	geliebt	*(Someone) loved me.*
du	wurdest	angerufen	*You got a telephone call.*
er/es/sie	wurde	gefüttert	*He/It/She was fed.*
wir	wurden	benachrichtigt	*We were informed.*
ihr	wurdet	überrascht	*You were surprised.*
sie/Sie	wurden	abgeholt	*They/You were picked up.*

- Present Perfect

The formation follows the same pattern as for all the other tenses: present perfect of werden (e. g. ich bin geworden) + past participle. There is just one small difference: in the passive we use worden instead of the normal past participle geworden.

	present tense of sein	+ past participle	+ worden	
ich	bin	geliebt	worden	*(Someone) loved me.*
du	bist	angerufen	worden	*You got a telephone call.*
er/es/sie	ist	gefüttert	worden	*He/It/She was fed.*
wir	sind	benachrichtigt	worden	*We were informed.*
ihr	seid	überrascht	worden	*You were surprised.*
sie/Sie	sind	abgeholt	worden	*They/You were picked up.*

• Past Perfect

	past simple of + sein	past participle	+ worden	
ich	war	geliebt	worden	*(Someone) had loved me.*
du	warst	angerufen	worden	*You had got a telephone call.*
er/es/sie	war	gefüttert	worden	*He/It/She had been fed.*
wir	waren	benachrichtigt	worden	*We had been informed.*
ihr	wart	überrascht	worden	*You had been surprised.*
sie/Sie	waren	abgeholt	worden	*They/You had been picked up.*

• Future Tense

	present tense of + werden	past participle	+ werden	
ich	werde	geliebt	werden	*(Someone) will love me.*
du	wirst	angerufen	werden	*You will get a telephone call.*
er/es/sie	wird	gefüttert	werden	*He/It/She will be fed.*
...				

• Future Perfect

	present tense of werden	+ past participle	+ worden sein	
ich	werde	geliebt	worden sein	*(Someone) will have loved me.*
du	wirst	angerufen	worden sein	*You will have got a telephone call.*
er/es/sie	wird	gefüttert	worden sein	*He/It/She will have been fed.*
...				

• Present Subjunctive

	present subjunctive of werden	+ past participle	
ich	werde	geliebt	*(that) (someone) loves me.*
er/es/sie	werde	gefüttert	*(that) he/it/she is being fed.*

• Past Subjunctive

	present subjunctive of werden	+ past participle	
ich	würde	geliebt	*(that) (someone) loved me.*
du	würdest	angerufen	*(that) you got a telephone call.*
er/es/sie	würde	gefüttert	*(that) he/it/she was being fed.*
...			

- Past Perfect Subjunctive

	past perfect subjunctive + of sein	past participle	+ worden	
ich	wäre	geliebt	worden	*(that) (someone) had/would have loved me.*
du	wärest	angerufen	worden	*You would have got a telephone call.*
er/es/sie	wäre	gefüttert	worden	*(that) he/it/she had/would have been fed.*
...				

- Passive of Modal Verbs

Do auxiliary verbs also have a passive form in German? Yes, of course they do – and when they occur there are all kinds of possibilities of forming a sentence.

The passive of modal verbs is formed like this:
modal verb form + past participle + werden in the infinitive

Marianne **soll** befördert **werden**.
(present)
Marianne is to be promoted.
Marianne **sollte befördert werden**.
(past simple)
Marianne was supposed to/should be promoted.
Marianne **hat befördert werden sollen**.
(present perfect)

Marianne was supposed to be promoted.
Marianne hatte befördert werden sollen.
(past perfect)
Marianne had been supposed to be promoted.
Marianne hätte befördert werden sollen.
(past subjunctive)
Marianne should have been promoted.

The present, past simple and past subjunctive are in common use. The present perfect and past perfect occur only very rarely.

12.2 Passiv-Alternativen
Alternatives for the Passive
oder Man baut das Regal so auf

If you want to remain impersonal but don't want to use the passive, then there are several alternatives you can use. Some of them are similar to English, others completely different.

(1) man
(2) sich lassen + infinitive
(3) ist, hat, gibt, bleibt, geht + zu + infinitive
(4) adjectives derived from verbs ending in -bar, -lich or -ig

passive	passive-alternative
(1) Was kann da gemacht werden? *What can be done?*	Was kann **man** da machen? *What can one do?*
(2) Das kann eingerichtet werden. *That can be arranged.*	Das **lässt sich** schon **einrichten**. *That can be arranged.*
(3) Es muss noch viel getan werden. *A lot still has to be done.*	Es **bleibt** noch viel **zu tun**. *A lot still remains to be done.*
(3) Diese Akte muss kopiert werden. *This file must be copied.*	Diese Akte **ist zu kopieren**. *This file is to be copied.*
(4) Dieses Vorgehen kann nicht vertreten werden. *This procedure can't be justified.*	Dieses Vorgehen ist nicht vertret**bar**. *This procedure is not justifiable.*
(4) Der Patient kann nicht transportiert werden. *The patient can't be moved.*	Der Patient ist nicht transportfäh**ig**. *The patient is not capable of being moved.*

12.3 Zustandspassiv   Passive Describing a State
oder *Das Regal ist aufgebaut*

Das Haus ist renoviert.

The house has been renovated.

There are two passive forms in German. Besides the passive describing actions or events, there is also the passive describing a state, a situation or a result (Zustandspassiv). The latter is not used as frequently.

Wir haben eine Stunde gearbeitet und jetzt **ist** das Regal **aufgebaut**. *We worked for an hour and now the shelves are up.*
Mein Schreibtisch **ist aufgeräumt**. *My desk is tidy.*
Die Haustür **ist** bereits **abgeschlossen**. *The front door is already locked.*

The passive describing a state occurs almost only in the present and past simple tenses. It is formed with the appropriate form of sein instead of werden.

(1) present tense: present tense of sein + past participle
(2) past simple: past simple of sein + past participle

(1) Manchmal wünsche ich mir, ich komme ins Büro, der Kaffee **ist** schon **gekocht**, alle meine Arbeit **ist** bereits **getan** und meine Chefin **ist verreist**. *Sometimes I wish that when I get into the office, the coffee has been made, all my work has already been done and my boss is away.*
(2) Ich träumte kürzlich, ich kam von der Arbeit nach Hause und das Geschirr **war abgespült**, alles **war aufgeräumt**, die Wäsche **war gewaschen** und **gebügelt** und das Essen **war gekocht** und stand auf dem Tisch. *I dreamt recently that I came home from work and the washing-up had been done, everything had been tidied away, the washing and ironing had been finished and supper had been cooked and was on the table.*

Exercise 22

Please form sentences using the passive in the past simple.

Example:

1990   Wiedervereinigung der beiden deutschen Staaten

1990 wurden die beiden deutschen Staaten wiedervereinigt.
....

a)   15. Jahrhundert   Druck der ersten Bücher in Europa

....

b)   in Frankfurt   Geburt von Johann Wolfgang von Goethe

....

c)   1895   Entdeckung der Röntgenstrahlen

....

d)   1957   Gründung der Europäischen Wirtschaftsgemeinschaft

....

e)   60er Jahre   Bau vieler Universitäten in Deutschland

....

f)   2002   Einführung des Euro

....

13 Präpositionen Prepositions
oder *Auf, über, für & Co.*

Sie kennen sich seit dem Kindergarten. They've known each other since playschool.

Prepositions come before nouns or groups of nouns and determine what case the noun needs to be in: accusative, dative or genitive.

⚡ Some prepositions combine with the definite article to form one single word (▶ **1.2** , p. 16 f.), e.g. zum = zu dem.

13.1 Präpositionen mit Akkusativ
Prepositions with Accusative
oder *Durch, für, gegen & Co.*

Some prepositions always take the accusative:

bis	**Bis nächsten Mittwoch** erwarte ich ein Ergebnis. *I expect a result by next Wednesday.* Er ist noch **bis einen Tag** nach Weihnachten in den USA. *He'll be in America till one day after Christmas.*

durch	Wir fahren gleich **durch einen langen Tunnel**. *In a minute we'll be driving through a long tunnel.* Unsere Firma geht zurzeit **durch eine schwierige Phase**. *Our firm is going through a difficult phase at the moment.*
für	Diese Rosen sind **für dich**. *These roses are for you.* Der Student bleibt **für drei Monate**. *The student is staying for three months.*
gegen	Frau Mino hat dieses Projekt **gegen den Willen** ihres Vorgesetzten durchgesetzt. *Frau Mino pushed this project through against her boss's will.* David ist mit dem Schlitten **gegen einen Baum** gefahren. *David crashed against a tree with his sledge.*
ohne	Herr Reyher hat die Rede **ohne seine Unterlagen** gehalten. *Herr Reyher made the speech without his notes.* Ich bin **ohne einen Cent** aus dem Haus gegangen. *I went out of the house without a cent.*
um	Nun rede doch nicht so **um den heißen Brei** herum. *Stop beating about the bush.* **Um die Ecke** ist ein Geldautomat. *There's a cash machine around the corner.*

Two other prepositions entlang and betreffend come after the noun. They don't occur very frequently.

Wir gehen den Strand **entlang** bis zum Hafen. *We'll go along the beach as far as the harbour.*
Den Vertrag **betreffend** wollten wir noch anmerken … *With reference to the contract we wanted to point out …*

⚡ The preposition bis is often used in combination with other prepositions which then determine the case.

Bis zum (dative) nächsten Mittwoch erwarte ich ein Ergebnis. *By next Wednesday I expect a result.*

13.2 Präpositionen mit Dativ
Prepositions with Dative
oder *Aus, bei, mit & Co.*

The following prepositions always take the dative case:

ab	**Ab nächster Woche** gehe ich regelmäßig schwimmen. *From next week on I'm going swimming regularly.* **Ab dem ersten August** ist Herr Radwan im Urlaub. *From the first of August Herr Radwan is on holiday.*
aus	Wir müssen die Sitzung **aus wichtigen Gründen** verschieben. *We must postpone the meeting for important reasons.* Michael kommt gerade **aus der Schule.** *Michael is just coming back from school.*
bei	Alan wohnt **bei seinem Freund.** *Alan is staying at his friend's house.* **Bei mir** gibt es so etwas nicht. *I don't have/ wouldn't do anything like that.*
gegen- über	**Gegenüber dem Firmengebäude** ist ein großer Park. *Opposite the office building is a large park.* **Gegenüber der Bank** ist ein Kiosk. *Opposite the bank there's a kiosk.*

mit	Raphael fährt **mit seinem Kollegen** zum Kongress. *Raphael is travelling with his colleague to the conference.*
	Wir machen unsere Arbeit **mit Spaß**. *We do our work with pleasure.*
nach	**Nach dem Mittagessen** muss ich zum Chef. *After lunch I have to go and see the boss.*
	Wir fahren am Wochenende **nach Paris**. *We're going to Paris at the weekend.*
seit	Carmen wohnt **seit vielen Jahren** in Bonn. *Carmen has been living in Bonn for many years.*
	Seit einer Woche warte ich auf Ihren Rückruf! *I've been waiting for you to answer my call for a week!*
von	Jonathan nimmt **vom ersten** bis zum zehnten Januar Urlaub. *Jonathan is having a holiday from the first till the tenth of January.*
	Unsere Kollegen kamen ganz begeistert **von der Messe** zurück. *Our colleagues came back from the fair full of enthusiasm.*
zu	Ich gratuliere dir **zur Gehaltserhöhung**! *Congratulations on your salary increase.*
	Laura musste **zum Zahnarzt** gehen. *Laura had to go to the dentist.*

13.3 Wechselpräpositionen **Varying Prepositions** oder *Akkusativ oder Dativ?*

There are some prepositions that can take more than just one case. They are called Wechselpräpositionen. They only indicate place or time:
an, auf, hinter, in, neben, über, unter, vor, zwischen.

1. Felix schubst den Ball an die Wand.
Felix is pushing the ball to the wall.

2. Der Ball liegt auf Felix' Nase.
The ball is on Felix's nose.

3. Der Ball liegt hinter Felix.
The ball is behind Felix.

4. Der Ball liegt neben Felix.
The ball is next to Felix.

5. Felix springt über den Ball.
Felix is jumping over the ball.

6. Der Ball liegt vor Felix.
The ball is in front of Felix.

7. Der Ball liegt unter Felix.
The ball is under Felix.

8. Felix steht zwischen den Bällen.
Felix is standing between the balls.

9. Felix und der Ball liegen im Korb.
Felix and the ball are lying in the basket.

It seems that these prepositions are not satisfied with exercising their influence in just one way. As a result they may choose the accusative or the dative case. There are rules, however, as to when and why.

Accusative is dynamic. It indicates movement: wohin *where to?* (ACTION)

Dative is static. It indicates place or movement within a limited place: wo *where?* (POSITION)

These examples will make things clear:

accusative: Wohin?	dative: Wo?
Wohin legst du die Akte?	Wo ist denn die Akte?
Where are you putting the file?	*Where is the file then?*
Ich lege/stelle die Akte …	Die Akte liegt/steht …
I'm putting it …	*The file is …*
an die Wand.	an der Wand.
up against the wall.	*up against the wall.*
auf den Tisch.	auf dem Tisch.
on the table.	*on the table.*
hinter das Telefon.	hinter dem Telefon.
behind the telephone.	*behind the telephone.*
in den Ablagekorb.	im Ablagekorb.
in the filing tray.	*in the filing tray.*
neben den Ordner.	neben dem Ordner.
next to the ring binder.	*next to the ring binder.*
über die Bücher.	über den Büchern.
above the books.	*above the books.*
unter die Bücher.	unter den Büchern.
under the books.	*under the books.*
vor das Buch.	vor dem Buch.
in front of the book.	*in front of the book.*
zwischen die anderen Akten.	zwischen den anderen Akten.
among the other files.	*among the other files.*

13.4 Präpositionen mit Genitiv
Prepositions with Genitive
oder *Wegen des Genitivs ...*

There are quite a few prepositions that take the genitive.
But nowadays they are used less and less. If they are
used in colloquial speech, people tend to prefer using the
dative instead. The most common prepositions taking the
genitive are as follows:

aufgrund	**Aufgrund der schlechten Umsatzzahlen** im ersten Quartal wurde eine Krisensitzung einberufen. *Due to the poor turnover figures in the first quarter a crisis meeting was called.*
statt	Ich hätte lieber Nudeln **statt (der) Kartoffeln.** *I'd rather have pasta instead of (the) potatoes.*
trotz	**Trotz des schlechten Wetters** fand das Fußballspiel statt. colloquial often: **Trotz dem schlechten Wetter** ... *In spite of the bad weather the football match took place.*
während	**Während des Meetings** ist Herr Maier fast eingeschlafen. colloquial often: **Während dem Meeting** ... *During the meeting Herr Maier almost fell asleep.*
wegen	Diana hat **wegen des Streits** mit ihrem Chef gekündigt. colloquial often: ... **wegen dem Streit** ... *Because of the dispute with her boss, Diana has resigned.*

Exercise 23

Please complete the following sentences using the correct case.

a) Die Abschlussfeier fand bei (mein Bruder Patrick) statt.

b) Der Autofahrer ist gegen (der Baum) gefahren.

c) Die Auszubildenden stehen im Kreis um (ihr Trainer).

d) Aufgrund (die Globalisierung) werden Sprachkenntnisse immer wichtiger.

e) Die Touristen-Information befindet sich gegenüber (das Rathaus).

f) Trotz (die zahlreichen Regeln) beherrscht Axel die deutsche Grammatik gut.

g) Seit (ein Jahr) hat Steve einen Job als Webdesigner.

h) Während (die Sommermonate) befinden sich im Bistro um die Ecke nur wenige Gäste.

i) Ramona ist am Wochenende zu (ihre Schwester) gefahren.

j) Der Bankangestellte holt das Geld aus (der Tresor).

k) Maggie und Geneviève haben für (der weltweite Friede) protestiert.

l) Der Schlüssel war zwischen (das Gepäck).

14 Satzverbindungen Sentence-Linkers
oder *Wie man Sätze verbindet*

KASSE

Sind Sie sicher, dass das der richtige Zettel ist?

x Milch
x Butter
x Shampoo
x Jack

Are you sure that's the right slip?

Although language bears little resemblance to a motor-bike, certain parts can be "bolted together" and taken apart again. It is possible to join several sentences together – not with nuts and bolts, but with little words called conjunctions. In German we divide these conjunctions into two groups: coordinating conjunctions (Konjunktionen) and subordinating conjunctions (Subjunktionen).

14.1 Konjunktionen Coordinating Conjunctions
oder *Und, aber, denn & Co.*

Coordinating conjunctions can join two sentences or main clauses together. The position of the verbs in both is the same.

conjunction	main focus of meaning	example
aber	limitation, contrast	Bitte verlegen Sie den Termin mit Herrn Manger auf nächste Woche, aber seien Sie bitte sehr freundlich! *Please postpone the appointment with Herr Manger till next week, but be nice about it.*
denn	reason	Peter ist übers Wochenende zu seinen Eltern gefahren, denn sein Vater wird 70. *Peter has gone to his parents for the weekend because it's his father's 70th birthday.*
doch	contrast	Wir wollten am Sonntag zum Surfen gehen, doch es hat leider den ganzen Tag geregnet. *We wanted to go surfing on Sunday, but unfortunately it rained all day.*
oder	alternative	Sollen wir zum Tauchen gehen oder wollen wir nur zum Baden fahren? *Shall we go diving or just go for a swim?*
sondern	alternative	Wir fliegen nicht nach Wien, sondern wir fahren mit dem Zug. *We're not flying to Vienna but travelling by train.*
und	enumeration	Alan ist jetzt schon zwei Monate in Deutschland und er fühlt sich sehr wohl hier. *Alan has been in Germany now for two months and he feels very much at home here.*

14.2 Subjunktionen
Subordinating Conjunctions
oder *Dass, weil & Co.*

Subordinating conjunctions connect a main clause with a subordinate clause. The subordinate clause can come before or after the main clause, but it can't stand on its own. Subordinate clauses have a different word order than main clauses (▶ ⑥, p. 67 ff.). All the verbs come at the end of the clause.

> Wir glauben, **dass** Sie das gut **verstehen können**.
> *We believe that you can understand that.*
> Ich frage mich, **ob** Sie das schon **verstanden haben**.
> *I wonder whether you understood that.*

Now it's not uncommon in German for several verbs to be used in one and the same sentence. When they occur in a subordinate clause, we have to ask ourselves how they can all be arranged in some sort of order.

• The conjugated verb comes right at the end:

> Eva freut sich, weil sie eine neue Stelle bekommen **hat**.
> *Eva is pleased because she's got a new job.*

• A participle or an infinitive comes directly before the conjugated verb:

> Ich komme, sobald ich diesen Text **fertig geschrieben habe.** *I'll come as soon as I've finished writing this text.*

• Separable verbs do not get separated:

> Herr Keller glaubt, dass seine Assistentin ihn **anlügt**.
> *Herr Keller believes that his assistant is lying to him.*

- When modal verbs are used in the present perfect
tense the conjugated verb comes before all the other
verb parts:

Timo erzählt stolz, dass er die Abschiedsrede für den
Chef **hat** halten dürfen. *Timo tells us proudly that he's
been allowed to make the farewell speech for the boss.*

The word order for the remaining elements in the clause
follows the same rules as in the main clause (▶ ⑥, p. 67).
There are a great many different types of subordinate
clauses *Nebensätze*. Relative clauses *Relativsätze*
and infinitive clauses *Infinitivsätze* will be dealt with
separately in the next few chapters because they don't
quite conform to the standard pattern. In the case of all
other subordinate clauses, the meaning (temporal or
causal) is comparatively easy to determine once you know
the meaning of the subordinating conjunction involved.

The most important subordinating conjunctions are:

con-junction	main focus of meaning	example
als	temporally simultaneous: point of time in the past	**Als** ich ins Büro kam, war meine Chefin schon da. *When I came into the office, my boss was already there.*
als	comparison	Das Projekt war schneller beendet, **als** wir erwartet hatten. *The project was finished faster than we had expected.*
als ob	unreal comparison	Er tat so, **als ob** er keine Zeit hätte. *He acted as if he had no time.*

con-junction	main focus of meaning	example
bevor	temporal	**Bevor** wir Pläne fürs Wochenende machen, möchte ich noch die Wettervorhersage hören. *Before we make any plans for the weekend, I'd like to hear the weather forecast.*
bis	temporal: end of an action	Wir warten noch, **bis** alle Teammitglieder da sind. *We're waiting until all team members are here.*
da	reason	**Da** Ralf und Anne zu viel Alkohol getrunken hatten, gingen sie lieber zu Fuß nach Hause. *Since Ralf and Anne had drunk too much alcohol, they preferred to walk home.*
damit	aim, purpose	Ich möchte sofort anfangen, **damit** wir pünktlich aufhören können. *I'd like to start immediately so we can finish on time.*
dass	aim, purpose, introduces a statement	Ich glaube, **dass** wir den Termin einhalten können. *I think that we can meet the deadline.*
nachdem	temporal	**Nachdem** ich beim Training gewesen war, ging es mir schon viel besser. *After I had done some training, I felt much better.*
ob	doubt, question, wondering	Ich weiß nicht, **ob** Paul schon zu Hause ist. *I don't know whether Paul is home yet.*

con-junction	main focus of meaning	example
obwohl	limitation	**Obwohl** das Wetter schlecht war, gingen wir spazieren. *Although the weather was bad, we went for a walk.*
seit(dem)	temporal	**Seit** Elena täglich Qigong macht, hat sie keine Kopfschmerzen mehr. *Since Elena has been doing Qi-gong every day, she doesn't have any more headaches.*
weil	reason	Wir kamen zu spät zur Präsentation, **weil** wir im Stau gestanden haben. *We arrived too late for the presentation because we were in a traffic jam.*
wenn	condition	**Wenn** du mal in Köln bist, musst du mich besuchen. *If you're ever in Cologne, you must come and visit me.*
(immer) wenn	temporal repeated action (in the past)	**(Immer) wenn** Maite in Deutschland war, hat sie uns besucht. *Whenever Maite was in Germany, she visited us.*

A subordinate clause can also be introduced by a question word (Fragewort). These clauses are called indirect questions (indirekte Fragesätze). (Question words ▷ **3.4**, p. 46 f.). This occurs mainly after a main clause containing verbs like sagen *to say*, fragen *to ask* or wissen *to know*.

Weißt du, **warum** Sylvia so schlechte Laune hat? *Do you know why Sylvia is in such a bad mood?*
Ich frage mich, **wo** meine Schlüssel sind. *I wonder where my keys are.*
Hast du verstanden, **was** sie gesagt hat? *Have you understood what she said?*

Exercise 24

Please combine the following sentences using the conjunctions in brackets.

a) Mike ist enttäuscht. Die Vergütung entspricht nicht seinen Vorstellungen. (weil)

b) Peer wirkt gelassen. Er macht täglich Yoga-Übungen. (seit)

c) Lucia spielt seit drei Jahren Gitarre. Sie surft auch gerne im Internet. (und)

d) Victor freut sich. Er kann nächste Woche in den Urlaub gehen. (dass)

e) Das Seminar fand nicht statt. Es gab zu wenig Teilnehmer. (da)

f) Frau Wilice besucht das Deutsche Museum. Sie geht auf den Marienplatz. (oder)

14.3 Relativsätze   Relative Clauses
oder *Sätze, die relativ häufig sind*

Haben Sie alle Fische alleine gefangen?

Nein, ich habe immer einen Wurm, der mir hilft.

Have you caught all the fish on your own? – No, I always have a worm to help me.

Relative clauses are introduced by a relative pronoun. A relative clause tells us more about a noun in the main clause. Normally the relative clause comes directly after the noun it describes.

main clause + main clause:

Judith verabredet sich mit einem Kollegen. Den Kollegen hat sie gestern in der Cafeteria kennengelernt. *Judith has a date with a colleague. She met the colleague in the cafeteria yesterday.*

main clause + relative clause:

Judith verabredet sich mit einem Kollegen, **den sie gestern in der Cafeteria kennengelernt hat**. *Judith has a date with a colleague whom she met in the cafeteria yesterday.*

Relative clauses often get inserted in the middle of a main clause:

> **Die Präsentation, die Frau Ronner gehalten hat, war sehr gut.** *The presentation that Frau Ronner held was very good.*

Apart from a few exceptions, the relative pronouns are identical to the definite article.

	masculine	neuter	feminine	plural
nom.	der	das	die	die
acc.	den	das	die	die
dat.	dem	dem	der	denen
gen.	dessen	dessen	deren	deren

 The correct form of the relative pronoun depends on two things. We might say that it faces in two directions.

It is the preceding noun being described in the relative clause that determines the gender (masculine, neuter or feminine) and the number (singular or plural), whereas the verb in the relative clause determines the case (nominative, accusative, dative or genitive).

Der Kollege, **den** ich schon lange kenne, hat heute gekündigt. *My colleague, whom I've known for a long time, handed in his notice today.*
accusative, masculine, singular

Die Kunden, **denen** du das Angebot geschickt hast, kommen morgen. *The customers you sent the offer to are coming tomorrow.*
dative, plural

Relative pronouns can also occur in combination with prepositions, in which case the preposition comes before the relative pronoun.

Das ist der Rucksack, **mit dem** ich schon die halbe Welt bereist habe. *That's the rucksack which I've toured half the world with.*
Da drüben ist eine Bäckerei, **in der** ich schon als Kind eingekauft habe. *Over there is a bakery where I've been a customer since I was a child.*
Wir kaufen eine Fahrkarte, **mit der** wir zu fünft fahren können. *We'll buy a ticket which all five of us can travel with.*

Relative pronouns in the genitive case replace the possessive article. No other article is then used with the noun that follows.

Die Kollegin, **deren** Hund immer mit ins Büro kommt, hat diese Woche Urlaub. *The colleague whose dog always comes with her to the office is on holiday this week.*
(**Ihr Hund** kommt immer mit ins Büro.) *(Her dog always comes with her to the office.)*
Der Mann, **dessen** Auto du beschädigt hast, ist jetzt hier. *The man whose car you damaged is here now.*
(Du hast **sein Auto** beschädigt.) *(You damaged his car.)*

Relative clauses can also refer to pronouns or to complete sentences. In these cases the relative pronoun is was.

Das ist alles, **was** ich dazu weiß. *That's all that I know about it.*

Das Wichtigste, **was** in so einem Fall getan werden sollte, ist ... *The most important thing that should be done in a case like this is ...*

Ich weiß nicht, **was** ich dazu noch sagen soll. *I don't know what to say to that.*

14.4 Infinitivsätze Infinitive Clauses
oder *Das ist leicht zu lernen*

Another type of subordinate clause is introduced without a normal conjunction. These are infinitive clauses with zu.

zu + infinitive

Infinitive clauses with zu + infinitive can be used after certain verbs, nouns or adjectives.

• Verbs with zu + infinitive

Here we have two groups of verbs. In the one group, the main clause and the subordinate clause both have the same subject. By using the zu + infinitive construction, we can avoid repetition.

zu + infinitive	alternative construction
Wir versuchen, Ihren Auftrag schnellstmöglich **zu bearbeiten**.	Wir versuchen, dass wir Ihren Auftrag schnellstmöglich bearbeiten.
We're trying to complete your order as quickly as possible.	
Hans meint, immer der Beste **sein zu müssen**.	Hans meint, er muss immer der Beste sein.
Hans believes he always needs to be the best.	
Denk daran, deine Medizin regelmäßig **zu nehmen**!	Denk daran, dass du deine Medizin regelmäßig nimmst.
Remember to take your medicine regularly.	

Other verbs in this group are:

anbieten	*to offer to*
anfangen	*to start to*
aufhören	*to stop*
beabsichtigen	*to intend to*
beginnen	*to begin to*
sich bemühen	*to make an effort to*
beschließen	*to decide to*
sich entschließen	*to decide to*
sich freuen	*to look forward to, be pleased to*
fürchten	*to fear to*
sich gewöhnen an	*to get used to*
glauben	*to believe*
hoffen	*to hope to*
planen	*to plan to*
scheinen	*to seem to*
vergessen	*to forget to*
sich verlassen auf	*to rely on sb. to*
versprechen	*to promise to*
vorhaben	*to intend to*
sich weigern	*to refuse to*

- In the second group of verbs, the zu + infinitive construction describes what the object of the sentence does.

Meine Freundin hat mich dazu überredet, mit ihr ins
Theater **zu gehen**. *My girlfriend has persuaded me to
go to the theatre with her.*
Peter hat Alan eingeladen, bei ihm **zu wohnen**. *Peter
has invited Alan to stay at his house.*
Jana fällt es nicht leicht, auf Schokolade **zu verzichten**.
It's not easy for Jana to do without chocolate.

Other verbs in this group are:

anbieten	*to offer to*
auffordern	*to ask sb. to*
befehlen	*to order sb. to*
bitten	*to ask sb. to*
bringen zu	*to bring sb. to*
empfehlen	*to recommend sb. to*
erinnern an	*to remind sb. to*
erlauben	*to permit sb. to*
ermöglichen	*to make it possible for sb. to*
gelingen	*to succeed in*
helfen	*to help sb. to*
hindern an	*to prevent sb. from*
raten	*to advise sb. to*
schwer fallen	*to have difficulty in*
verbieten	*to forbid sb. to*
warnen vor	*to warn sb. about*

⚡ Verbs with a separable prefix have the zu in the middle – between prefix and main stem.

Eva freut sich darauf, mit Alan und Peter aus**zu**gehen. (ausgehen) *Eva is looking forward to going out with Alan and Peter.*
Christa hat ihrer Nachbarin angeboten, für sie ein**zu**kaufen. (einkaufen) *Christa has offered her neighbour to do her shopping for her.*
Dem Team gelang es, ein sensationelles Angebot aus**zu**arbeiten. (ausarbeiten) *The team succeeded in working out a sensational offer.*

• Nouns with zu + infinitive

Die Kinder haben keine **Lust**, ihre Zimmer **aufzuräumen**.
The children don't feel like tidying up their rooms.
Elisabeth hat die **Absicht**, die Stelle **zu wechseln**.
Elisabeth intends to change her job.
Helmut hatte kein **Problem**, sich mit den Leuten in
Peru **zu verständigen**. *Helmut had no problem in
communicating with the people in Peru.*

Further nouns followed by zu + infinitive are:

die Angst	*fear (of)*
die Freude	*joy, pleasure (in)*
die Gelegenheit	*opportunity (to/of)*
der Grund	*reason (to)*
die Möglichkeit	*possibility (of)*
die Mühe	*effort, trouble (to)*
das Problem	*problem (in)*
die Schwierigkeiten	*difficulty (in)*
der Spaß	*fun (in)*
die Zeit	*time (to)*

• Adjectives and participles with zu + infinitive

These adjectives or participles normally come after a
form of the verb sein *to be* or finden *to find*.

Es **ist** gesund, viel Gemüse und Obst **zu essen**. *It's
healthy to eat lots of vegetables and fruit.*
Viele Leute **finden** es unhöflich, ohne Entschuldigung
deutlich zu spät **zu kommen**. *Many people find it
impolite to arrive much too late without an apology.*

Further adjectives and participles of this kind are:

bereit	*ready (to)*
entschlossen	*determined (to)*
erlaubt/verboten	*permitted/forbidden (to)*
erfreut	*pleased (to)*
erstaunt	*amazed (to)*
falsch/richtig	*wrong/right (to)*
gewohnt	*accustomed/used (to)*
gut/schlecht	*good/bad (to)*
interessant/uninteressant	*interesting/uninteresting (to)*
nötig/unnötig	*necessary/unnecessary (to)*
praktisch/unpraktisch	*practical/impractical (to)*
stolz	*proud (to)*
überzeugt	*convinced (about)*
wichtig/unwichtig	*important/unimportant (to)*

• um + zu + infinitive

Sentences with um + zu + infinitive express a purpose or an aim in the same way as subordinate clauses with the conjunction damit. If the subject of the main clause and the subordinate clause are identical, we can use the um + zu + infinitive construction. Otherwise we have to use damit.

um + zu + infinitive	damit
Wir haben in dieser Sitzung keine Zeit, **um** über so ein Thema **zu diskutieren**. *We don't have time in this meeting to discuss such a topic.*	Wir haben diese Sitzung nicht einberufen, **damit** Sie dieses unwichtige Thema diskutieren. *We haven't called this meeting so that you can discuss this unimportant topic.*
Paula ist gekommen, **um** uns beim Umzug **zu helfen**. *Paula has come to help us with the move.*	Paula ist gekommen, **damit** Laura die Arbeit nicht allein machen muss. *Paula has come so that Laura doesn't have to do the work on her own.*
Sina arbeitet im Kino, **um** ihr Taschengeld **aufzubessern**. *Sina is working at the cinema to earn some more pocket money.*	Sina arbeitet im Kino, **damit** die ganze Familie Freikarten bekommt. *Sina is working at the cinema so her whole family can get free tickets.*

⚡ Here, too, separable verbs have the zu in the middle.

Leo ist auf den Markt gegangen, **um** ein**zu**kaufen. *Leo has gone to the market to do some shopping.*
Wir sind ins Naturkundemuseum gegangen, **um** uns die Saurierskelette an**zu**sehen. *We went to the Natural History Museum to see the dinosaur skeletons.*

15 Wortbildung   Word Formation
oder *Aus zwei mach vier*

Herr Ober, haben Sie mich vergessen?

Nein, nein. Sie sind der Schweine-braten.

Waiter, have you forgotten me? – No, you're the roast pork.

One thing you'll like about German is the fact that you can increase your vocabulary by using the rules of word formation. New composite words can be created by combining two or more single ones or by adding prefixes or suffixes. This happens all the time and new combinations can occur daily.

If you come across a long complicated-looking word that you don't understand, it often helps if you split it up into its constituent parts. You'll probably understand each of these more easily. Then read these single elements in reverse order and the meaning of the whole word will become clear.

Thus a Schweine/hals/braten is a Braten *roast* from the Hals *neck* of a Schwein *pig* and Semmel/knödel are Knödel *dumplings* made from Semmeln (Bavarian word for) *bread rolls*.

15.1 Komposition   Composing New Words
oder *Fassbier und Flaschenwein*

No matter how many elements the compound word has, it is always the last element that determines what kind of word it is. In the case of nouns, the last element determines the gender. The preceding elements tell us more about it. They define the basic word.

der Flaschenwein
defining word + basic word
wine from a bottle (and not from a barrel)
die Weinflasche
defining word + basic word
a bottle of wine (and not a glass)

⚡ The meaning of a compound word does not necessarily correspond with the meaning of its constituent parts. A Kindergarten is not a Garten *garden* for Kinder *children*, but a play school for very young children.

Word composition like this occurs most often with nouns, but can also take place with other kinds of words.

• Noun + Noun

die Steuer + **der** Berater = **der** Steuerberater
tax + advisor = tax advisor
die Liebe + **der** Kummer = **der** Liebeskummer
love + worries = trouble with your love life
der Traum + **der** Job = **der** Traumjob
dream + job = dream job

• Adjective + Noun

rot + **der** Wein = **der** Rotwein
red + wine = red wine
groß + **die** Stadt = **die** Großstadt
big + town = city
weich + **das** Ei = **das** Weichei
soft + egg = softy, weakling

• Noun + Adjective

das Vitamin + reich = vitaminreich
vitamin + rich = rich in vitamins
die Umwelt + schonend = umweltschonend
environment + treating with care = environmentally friendly
das Bild + schön = bildschön
picture + beautiful = pretty as a picture
die Medien + wirksam = medienwirksam
media + effective = to great effect in the media

• Verb + Noun

schlafen + **das** Zimmer = **das** Schlafzimmer
sleep + room = bedroom
tanzen + **die** Schuhe = **die** Tanzschuhe
dance + shoes = dancing shoes
boxen + **die** Handschuhe = **die** Boxhandschuhe
box + gloves = boxing gloves

- Preposition + Noun

vor + **der** Vertrag = **der** Vorvertrag
before + contract = provisional contract
nach + **die** Sicht = **die** Nachsicht
after + sight = tolerance
innen + **die** Politik = **die** Innenpolitik
inner + politics = home affairs

- Adjective + Adjective

dunkel + rot = dunkelrot
dark + red = dark red
hell + blond = hellblond
light + blond = light-blond

- Adverb + Verb

wieder + sehen = wiedersehen
again + see = meet again

Often several of the above word types are combined. In principle, anything is possible, provided you can remember at the end of the word what the beginning was. Examples:

die Mit/fahr/gelegenheit *chance of a lift*
die Mit/wohn/zentrale *flat sharing agency*
der Vor/stands/vor/sitzende *Chairman of the Board, Chief Executive*
die Mit/arbeiter/versammlung *staff meeting*

And, of course, the now very famous tongue-in-cheek example:

Donaudampfschifffahrtsgesellschaftskapitänskajüten-türschloss *The lock on the cabin door of the captain from the Danube steamship company*

⚡ A lot of compound nouns refuse to fit together without a little help. They need something to seal the join:

die Arbeit + der Markt = der Arbeit**s**markt
work + market = labour market
der Aufwand + die Entschädigung =
die Aufwand**s**entschädigung
effort + compensation = compensation for work involved

Quite a lot of compounds make use of the plural rather than the singular.

die Aprikosen (plural) + die Marmelade =
die Aprikosenmarmelade
(You need more than one apricot.)
apricots + jam = apricot jam
die Kinder (plural) + der Garten = der Kindergarten
(There's always more than one child.)
children + garden = kindergarten

Exercise 25

Please form compound words from the following and then add the correct form of the definite article.

a) Baum + Gummi   ....

b) Ordner + Ring   ....

c) Papier + Drucker   ....

d) Schalter + Licht   ....

e) Läufer + schnell   ....

f) Wohnung + Markt   ....

g) über + Bevölkerung   ....

h) Tasche + Handy   ....

i) nass + Schnee   ....

j) blau + hell   ....

k) Abend + vor   ....

15.2 Derivation   Deriving New Words
oder *Verständlich und lernbar*

We can derive new words by adding a prefix or a suffix to an existing basic element. The kind of word can vary. In the case of verbs, the infinitive ending often disappears.

programmieren – der Programmier**er** – die Programmier**erin**
to program – male programmer – female programmer
frei + **-heit** = die Freiheit
free – freedom
fahren – die Fahrt
to travel – journey
bewegen + **-ung** = die Bewegung
to move – movement
der Sommer + **-lich** = sommerlich
summer – summery
der Frühling + **-(s)haft** = frühlingshaft
spring – spring-like
be + arbeiten = bearbeiten
to work – to work on something

- Prefixes are often used with verbs, e.g. ankommen *to arrive*, durchlesen *to read through*, wiederholen *to repeat*. ▷ **7.3** , p. 82 ff. With nouns and adjectives we very often find the prefixes in- and un-. They turn the noun into its negative form or its opposite.

das Unglück (kein Glück)	*calamity, misfortune (no luck)*
unglücklich (nicht glücklich usw.)	*unhappy (not happy)*
der Unsinn	*nonsense*
unsinnig	nonsensical, silly
unfreundlich	*unfriendly, rude*
die Inkompetenz	*incompetence*
inkompetent	*incompetent*
insolvent	*insolvent, bankrupt*
die Instabilität	*instability*

- Suffixes are used to form new nouns or adjectives. As a result, new words are formed on the basis of other nouns, verbs or adjectives. In the case of nouns, the suffix will determine the gender of the new noun (▷ **2.1** , p. 21 ff.).

gesund + **-heit** = die Gesundheit
healthy – health
fröhlich + **-keit** = die Fröhlichkeit
good-humoured – good-humour
bearbeiten + **-ung** = die Bearbeitung
to work on something – the actual work itself
der Wunsch + **-los** = wunschlos
wish – without a wish (completely satisfied)
leben + **-haft** = lebhaft
to live – lively
der Wind + **-ig** = windig
wind – windy

Exercise 26

Please add the missing prefixes and suffixes.

a) Simons Katze ist ....laufen.

b) Herr Franklin muss noch ....checken.

c) Marilyn ist krank und sollte sich daher ....decken.

d) Die Reisefrei........ war als wichtiger Fortschritt zu betrachten.

e) Das Bungee-Jumping sieht gefähr........ aus.

f) Frau Setlur macht einen jugend........ Eindruck.

g) Wir müssen das Geschenk ....packen.

h) Sollen wir Sie das Stück ....nehmen?

i) Auf dieses Angebot werden Sie bestimmt noch ....kommen.

j) Die Freund........ mit Jenny war mir viel wert.

k) Die Assistent........ stellte das Projekt fertig.

l) Wir hoffen, dass Sie jetzt nicht mehr sprach........ sind!

Now it's time to say goodbye! We wish you every success for your future German studies. Have lots of fun!

Unregelmäßige und gemischte Verben
Irregular and Mixed Verbs

The most important irregular and mixed verbs are listed alphabetically in the following tables. Mixed verbs are marked with an *.

All verbs are listed in groups according to the vowel changes they undergo in their different tenses (see **9.2**).

infinitive	present tense	past simple	present perfect	translation
A – B – A				
blasen	bläst	blies	hat geblasen	*to blow*
braten	brät	briet	hat gebraten	*to roast*
empfangen	empfängt	empfing	hat empfangen	*to receive*
fallen	fällt	fiel	ist gefallen	*to fall*
fangen	fängt	fing	hat gefangen	*to catch*
geraten	gerät	geriet	ist geraten	*to fall/get into*
hängen	hängt	hing	hat gehangen	*to hang*
halten	hält	hielt	hat gehalten	*to stop, hold*
lassen	lässt	ließ	hat gelassen	*to let, leave, stop*
raten	rät	riet	hat geraten	*to guess*
schlafen	schläft	schlief	hat geschlafen	*to sleep*
laufen	läuft	lief	ist gelaufen	*to run*
heißen	heißt	hieß	hat geheißen	*to be called*
stoßen	stößt	stieß	hat gestoßen	*to push, knock*
rufen	ruft	rief	hat gerufen	*to call*

infinitive	present tense	past simple	present perfect	translation
backen	bäckt (backt)	buk (backte)	hat gebacken	to bake
fahren	fährt	fuhr	hat/ist gefahren	to drive, travel
graben	gräbt	grub	hat gegraben	to dig
laden	lädt	lud	hat geladen	to load
schaffen	schafft	schuf	hat geschaffen	to create, do
schlagen	schlägt	schlug	hat geschlagen	to hit, beat
tragen	trägt	trug	hat getragen	to carry, to wear
wachsen	wächst	wuchs	ist gewachsen	to grow
waschen	wäscht	wusch	hat gewaschen	to wash
essen	isst	aß	hat gegessen	to eat (of people)
fressen	frisst	fraß	hat gefressen	to eat (of animals)
geben	gibt	gab	hat gegeben	to give
geschehen	geschieht	geschah	ist geschehen	to happen
lesen	liest	las	hat gelesen	to read
messen	misst	maß	hat gemessen	to measure
sehen	sieht	sah	hat gesehen	to see
treten	tritt	trat	hat/ist getreten	to step, kick
vergessen	vergisst	vergaß	hat vergessen	to forget
A – B – B				
*brennen	brennt	brannte	hat gebrannt	to burn
*bringen	bringt	brachte	hat gebracht	to bring, fetch, take
*denken	denkt	dachte	hat gedacht	to think

infinitive	present tense	past simple	present perfect	translation
*kennen	kennt	kannte	hat gekannt	*to know (be acquainted)*
*nennen	nennt	nannte	hat genannt	*to name, call*
*rennen	rennt	rannte	ist gerannt	*to run, race*
*senden	sendet	sandte (sendete)	hat gesandt (gesendet)	*to send*
stehen	steht	stand	hat/ist gestanden	*to stand*
beweisen	beweist	bewies	hat bewiesen	*to prove*
bleiben	bleibt	blieb	ist geblieben	*to stay, remain*
gedeihen	gedeiht	gedieh	ist gediehen	*to flourish*
leihen	leiht	lieh	hat geliehen	*to lend*
meiden	meidet	mied	hat gemieden	*to avoid*
preisen	preist	pries	hat gepriesen	*to praise*
reiben	reibt	rieb	hat gerieben	*to rub*
scheiden	scheidet	schied	hat/ist geschieden	*to separate*
scheinen	scheint	schien	hat geschienen	*to seem, to shine*
schmeißen	schmeißt	schmiss	hat geschmissen	*to throw, hurl*
schreiben	schreibt	schrieb	hat geschrieben	*to write*
schreien	schreit	schrie	hat geschrien	*to scream, cry*
schweigen	schweigt	schwieg	hat geschwiegen	*to stay silent*
steigen	steigt	stieg	ist gestiegen	*to climb, to rise*
treiben	treibt	trieb	hat getrieben	*to drive, drift, do*
verzeihen	verzeiht	verzieh	hat verziehen	*to forgive*
weisen	weist	wies	hat gewiesen	*to direct, show*

infinitive	present tense	past simple	present perfect	translation
beißen	beißt	biss	hat gebissen	*to bite*
gleichen	gleicht	glich	hat geglichen	*to be similar to, same as*
gleiten	gleitet	glitt	ist geglitten	*to glide*
greifen	greift	griff	hat gegriffen	*to grab, grip*
kneifen	kneift	kniff	hat gekniffen	*to pinch*
leiden	leidet	litt	hat gelitten	*to suffer*
pfeifen	pfeift	pfiff	hat gepfiffen	*to whistle*
reißen	reißt	riss	hat/ist gerissen	*to tear, break*
reiten	reitet	ritt	hat/ist geritten	*to ride*
schleichen	schleicht	schlich	ist geschlichen	*to slide, slip, slink*
schneiden	schneidet	schnitt	hat geschnitten	*to cut*
schreiten	schreitet	schritt	ist geschritten	*to step*
streichen	streicht	strich	hat gestrichen	*to spread, paint, cut out*
streiten	streitet	stritt	hat gestritten	*to quarrel, argue*
weichen	weicht	wich	ist gewichen	*to give way, move*
heben	hebt	hob	hat gehoben	*to lift, raise*
biegen	biegt	bog	hat/ist gebogen	*to bend*
bieten	bietet	bot	hat geboten	*to offer*
erwägen	erwägt	erwog	hat erwogen	*to consider*
fliegen	fliegt	flog	hat/ist geflogen	*to fly*
fliehen	flieht	floh	ist geflohen	*to flee*
fließen	fließt	floss	ist geflossen	*to flow*

infinitive	present tense	past simple	present perfect	translation
frieren	friert	fror	hat gefroren	*to freeze*
genießen	genießt	genoss	hat genossen	*to enjoy*
gießen	gießt	goss	hat gegossen	*to pour*
kriechen	kriecht	kroch	ist gekrochen	*to crawl*
riechen	riecht	roch	hat gerochen	*to smell*
schieben	schiebt	schob	hat geschoben	*to push*
schießen	schießt	schoss	hat/ist geschossen	*to shoot*
schließen	schließt	schloss	hat geschlossen	*to close*
sprießen	sprießt	spross	ist gesprossen	*to sprout*
verlieren	verliert	verlor	hat verloren	*to lose*
wiegen	wiegt	wog	hat gewogen	*to weigh*
ziehen	zieht	zog	hat/ist gezogen	*to pull*
*wissen	weiß	wusste	hat gewusst	*to know (facts)*
*können	kann	konnte	hat gekonnt	*to be able (can)*
*mögen	mag	mochte	hat gemocht	*to like*
betrügen	betrügt	betrog	hat betrogen	*to deceive*
lügen	lügt	log	hat gelogen	*to lie*
*müssen	muss	musste	hat gemusst	*to have to (must)*
*dürfen	darf	durfte	hat gedurft	*to be allowed to / (may)*
A – B – C				
befehlen	befiehlt	befahl	hat befohlen	*to order, instruct*
bergen	birgt	barg	hat geborgen	*to save, rescue, recover*

infinitive	present tense	past simple	present perfect	translation
bewerben	bewirbt	bewarb	hat beworben	*to apply (for)*
brechen	bricht	brach	hat/ist gebrochen	*to break*
empfehlen	empfiehlt	empfahl	hat empfohlen	*to recommend*
erschrecken	erschrickt	erschrak	hat/ist erschrocken	*to frighten, be frightened*
gelten	gilt	galt	hat gegolten	*to be valid, to count*
helfen	hilft	half	hat geholfen	*to help*
nehmen	nimmt	nahm	hat genommen	*to take*
sprechen	spricht	sprach	hat gesprochen	*to speak*
stechen	sticht	stach	hat gestochen	*to sting, bite, stab*
stehlen	stiehlt	stahl	hat gestohlen	*to steal*
sterben	stirbt	starb	ist gestorben	*to die*
treffen	trifft	traf	hat getroffen	*to meet, to hit*
verderben	verdirbt	verdarb	hat/ist verdorben	*to spoil*
werben	wirbt	warb	hat geworben	*to advertise*
werfen	wirft	warf	hat geworfen	*to throw*
beginnen	beginnt	begann	hat begonnen	*to begin*
gewinnen	gewinnt	gewann	hat gewonnen	*to win*
schwimmen	schwimmt	schwamm	hat/ist geschwommen	*to swim*
bitten	bittet	bat	hat gebeten	*to ask, request*
liegen	liegt	lag	hat gelegen	*to lie (position)*
sitzen	sitzt	saß	hat/ist gesessen	*to sit*
binden	bindet	band	to bind, tie	*to bind, tie*

infinitive	present tense	past simple	present perfect	translation
dringen	dringt	drang	ist gedrungen	*to push through*
empfinden	empfindet	empfand	hat empfunden	*to feel*
finden	findet	fand	hat gefunden	*to find*
gelingen	gelingt	gelang	ist gelungen	*to succeed*
klingen	klingt	klang	hat geklungen	*to sound*
misslingen	misslingt	misslang	ist misslungen	*to fail*
ringen	ringt	rang	hat gerungen	*to wrestle*
schlingen	schlingt	schlang	hat geschlungen	*to tie, wrap*
schwingen	schwingt	schwang	hat geschwungen	*to swing*
singen	singt	sang	hat gesungen	*to sing*
sinken	sinkt	sank	ist gesunken	*to sink*
springen	springt	sprang	ist gesprungen	*to jump*
stinken	stinkt	stank	hat gestunken	*to stink*
trinken	trinkt	trank	hat getrunken	*to drink*
zwingen	zwingt	zwang	hat gezwungen	*to force*
andere Verben				
*haben	hat	hatte	hat gehabt	*to have*
sein	ist	war	ist gewesen	*to be*
*sollen	soll	sollte	hat gesollt	*to be supposed to*
*wollen	will	wollte	hat gewollt	*to want*
tun	tut	tat	hat getan	*to do*
kommen	kommt	kam	ist gekommen	*to come*
werden	wird	wurde	ist geworden	*to become*
gehen	geht	ging	ist gegangen	*to go*

Wichtigste Dativ-Verben
Most Important Verbs Taking Dative

Verbs with Dative only	
ähneln	*to look like, be similar to*
auffallen	*to be noticeable (to sb.)*
antworten	*to answer*
befehlen	*to order, instruct*
begegnen	*to meet*
beistehen	*to stand by, support sb.*
danken	*to thank*
einfallen	*to occur (to sb.)*
entgegnen	*to reply, retort, counter*
erscheinen	*to appear*
erwidern	*to reply*
fehlen	*to miss, be missing*
folgen	*to follow*
gefallen	*to please*
gehören	*to belong*
gehorchen	*to obey*
gelingen	*to succeed*
genügen	*to satisfy, be enough*
glauben	*to believe (sb.)*
gratulieren	*to congratulate*
helfen	*to help*
misslingen	*to fail*
sich nähern	*to approach*
nützen	*to be useful*

Verbs with Dative only

passen	to suit
raten	to advise
schaden	to harm, damage
schmecken	to taste
vertrauen	to trust
verzeihen	to forgive
(aus)weichen	to avoid
widersprechen	to contradict
zuhören	to listen
zureden	to persuade, encourage
zusagen	to accept, confirm, approve
zuschauen	to watch
zusehen	to watch
zustimmen	to agree
zuwenden	to devote (to), bestow (on)

Verbs with Dative and Accusative

anvertrauen	to entrust sb. with sth.
beantworten	to answer sb. sth.
beweisen	to prove sth. to sb.
borgen	to borrow, lend sth. to sb.
bringen	to bring, take, fetch sb. sth.
empfehlen	to recommend sth. to sb.
entwenden	to remove, steal sth. from sb.
entziehen	to withdraw sth. from sb.
erlauben	to permit, allow sth. to sb.
erzählen	to tell, narrate sb. sth.

Verbs with Dative and Accusative

geben	*to give sb. sth.*
leihen	*to lend sb. sth.*
liefern	*to deliver sth. to sb.*
melden	*to report sth. to sb.*
mitteilen	*to inform sb. of sth.*
nehmen	*to take sb. sth.*
rauben	*to rob sb. of sth.*
sagen	*to say sth. to sb.*
schenken	*to give sb. sth. (as a present)*
schicken	*to send sb. sth.*
schreiben	*to write sth. to sb.*
schulden	*to owe sb. sth.*
senden	*to send sb. sth.*
stehlen	*to steal sth. from sb.*
überlassen	*to relinquish, let sb. have sth.*
verbieten	*to forbid sb. to do sth.*
verschweigen	*to keep quiet about sth. to sb.*
versprechen	*to promise sb. sth.*
verweigern	*to refuse sb. sth.*
verzeihen	*to forgive sb. sth.*
vorlesen	*to read sth. out loud to sb.*
vorwerfen	*to accuse, blame sb. of sth.*
wegnehmen	*to take sth. away from sb.*
zeigen	*to show sb. sth.*

Verben mit festen Präpositionen
Phrasal Verbs

abhängen	von + D(ativ)	*to depend on*
sich amüsieren	über + A(kkusativ)	*to be amused about*
achten	auf + A	*to pay attention to*
anfangen	mit + D	*to begin with*
ankommen	auf + A	*to depend on*
antworten	auf + A	*to answer*
sich ärgern	über + A	*to be annoyed about*
aufhören	mit + D	*to stop doing*
aufpassen	auf + A	*to look after*
sich aufregen	über + A	*to get excited about*
ausgeben	für + A	*to spend on*
sich bedanken	bei + D; für + A	*to thank sb. for*
beginnen	mit + D	*to begin with*
sich bemühen	um + A	*to try to get/take trouble over*
berichten	über + A	*to report on*
sich beschäftigen	mit + D	*to busy oneself with*
sich beschränken	auf + A	*to limit oneself to*
sich beschweren	bei + D; über + A	*to complain to sb. about*
bestehen	aus + D	*to consist of*
bestellen	für + A	*to order for*
bestrafen	für + A	*to punish for*
sich beteiligen	an + D	*to take part in/have a share in*
sich bewerben	um + A	*to apply for*

sich beziehen	auf + A	*to refer to*
bitten	um + A	*to ask for*
brauchen	zu + D	*to need*
danken	für + A	*to thank for*
denken	an + A	*to think of*
diskutieren	über + A	*to discuss, talk about*
einladen	zu + D	*to invite to*
sich entscheiden	für + A	*to decide on*
sich entschließen	zu + D	*to decide to*
sich entschuldigen	bei + D; für + A	*to apologise to sb. for*
erfahren	durch + A	*to learn from/ through*
sich erholen	von + D	*to recover from*
sich erinnern	an + A	*to remember*
erkennen	an + D	*to recognise in*
sich erkundigen	nach + D	*to enquire about*
erzählen	von + D	*to tell (a story) about*
fehlen	an + D	*to be missing*
fragen	nach + D	*to ask after/about*
sich freuen	auf + A	*to look forward to*
sich freuen	über + A	*to be pleased about*
führen	zu + D	*to lead to*
gehen	um + A	*to involve*
gehören	zu + D	*to belong to*
sich gewöhnen	an + A	*to get used to*
glauben	an + A	*to believe in*
gratulieren	zu + D	*to congratulate on*
halten	für + A	*to consider to be*
halten	von + D	*to have an opinion of/on*

sich halten	an + A	*to comply with*
handeln	von + D	*to involve, have to do with*
helfen	bei + D	*to help in*
hindern	an + D	*to prevent from*
hinweisen	auf + A	*to point out*
hoffen	auf + A	*to hope for*
hören	von + D	*to hear from/about*
sich informieren	über + A	*to find out about*
sich interessieren	für + A	*to be interested in*
interessiert sein	an + D	*to be interested in*
sich konzentrieren	auf + A	*to concentrate on*
kämpfen	für + A	*to fight for*
klagen	über + A	*to complain about*
kommen	zu + D	*to come to*
sich kümmern	um + A	*to take care of*
lachen	über + A	*to laugh at/about*
leiden	an + D	*to suffer from*
leiden	unter + D	*to suffer from, have problems with*
liegen	an + D	*to be due to (cause)*
nachdenken	über + A	*to think about*
profitieren	von + D	*to profit from*
protestieren	gegen + A	*to protest against*
rechnen	mit + D	*to reckon on/with*
reden	über + A	*to talk about*
reden	von + D	*to talk of*
riechen	nach + D	*to smell of*
sagen	über + A	*to say about*
sagen	zu + D	*to say to*
schicken	zu + D	*to send to*
schmecken	nach + D	*to taste of*

schreiben	an + A	to write to
sich schützen	vor + D	to protect oneself from
sehen	von + D	to see of
sein	für + A	to be for
sein	gegen + A	to be against
senden	an + A	to send to
sorgen	für + A	to care for, look after
sprechen	mit + D; über + A	to speak to sb. about
sterben	an + D	to die of
suchen	nach + D	to look for
teilnehmen	an + D	to take part in
telefonieren	mit + D	to telephone sb.
träumen	von + D	to dream of
sich trennen	von + D	to part from/with
sich überzeugen	von + D	to convince oneself about
sich unterhalten	mit + D; über + A	to have a conversation with sb. about
sich unterscheiden	von + D	to differ from
sich verabreden	für + A; mit + D	to arrange to meet on/at … with
sich verabschieden	von + D	to say goodbye to
verbinden	mit + D	to connect with
vergleichen	mit + D	to compare with/to
sich verlassen	auf + A	to rely on
sich verlieben	in + A	to fall in love with
sich verständigen	mit + D	to communicate with
verstehen	von + D	to understand about

sich verstehen	mit + D	*to get on well with*
sich vorbereiten	auf + A	*to prepare to/for*
sich vorstellen	bei + D	*to have an interview with*
warnen	vor + D	*to warn about*
warten	auf + A	*to wait for*
sich wenden	an + A	*to turn to*
werden	zu + D	*to become*
wissen	von + D	*to know of*
sich wundern	über + A	*to wonder about*
zweifeln	an + D	*to have doubts about*
zwingen	zu + D	*to force, compel to*

Terminologie **Terminology**

Englisch	Deutsch	Beispiel
Accusative (acc.)	Akkusativ	*den* Weg kennen
Active (voice)	Aktiv	ich *füttere* die Katze
Adjective	Adjektiv	eine *blaue* Hose
Adverb	Adverb	sie gingen *langsam*
Auxiliary verb	Hilfsverb	ich *habe* gesungen
Case	Kasus	Nominativ, Genitiv, Dativ, Akkusativ
Comparative	Komparativ	ein *schöneres* Auto, sie fuhren *schneller*
Compound word	Kompositum	Deutschlehrer, Arbeitsmarktsituation
Conjugation	Konjugation	ich *fahre*, du *fährst*
Conjunction	Konjunktion	wir aßen *und* tranken
Dative (dat.)	Dativ	sie glaubt *mir*
Declension (of nouns, articles, pronouns and adjectives)	Deklination (von Substantiven, Artikel, Pronomen und Adjektiven)	des nett*en* Mannes
Definite article	bestimmter Artikel	*der, die, das*
Demonstrative pronoun	Demonstrativpronomen	*dieser* Junge
Direct speech	direkte Rede	Er sagt: *"Du bist schön."*
Feminine	Feminin	*die* Bluse, *eine* Rose
Future tense	Futur	ich *werde lernen*
Future perfect tense	Futur II	ich *werde gelernt haben*
Gender	Genus	*das* Mädchen, *der* Garten
Genitive (gen.)	Genitiv	*des* Vaters, *der* Mutter, *des* Kindes

Englisch	Deutsch	Beispiel
Imperative	Imperativ	*gib* es mir!
Indefinite article	unbestimmter Artikel	*ein, eine*
Indefinite pronoun	Indefinitpronomen	*jeder, einige, irgendein*
Indicative	Indikativ	wir *lernen*, du *kamst*
Indirect speech	indirekte Rede	Er sagt, *sie sei schön.*
Infinitive	Infinitiv	*spielen, reden*
Interrogative pronoun	Interrogativ- pronomen	*wer, wo*
Masculine	Maskulin	*der* Anzug, *ein* Baum
Modal particle	Modalpartikel	*eigentlich, halt, eben*
Modal verb	Modalverb	können, müssen, wollen
Mood	Modus	ich *gehe*, ich *ginge*, *geh*!
Neuter	Neutrum	*das* Haus, *ein* Buch
Nominative (nom.)	Nominativ	*der* Mann, *die* Frau, *das* Kind
Noun	Substantiv	*Sonne, Glück*
Number	Numerus	Singular, Plural
Object	Objekt	Maria kauft *Schuhe.*
Passive (voice)	Passiv	die Katze *wird gefüttert*
Past participle	Partizip Perfekt (Partizip II)	*gefahren, verkauft*
Past perfect	Plusquamperfekt	ich *hatte gelesen*
Past subjunctive	Konjunktiv II (= Konjunktiv Imperfekt)	er *wäre müde*
Past tense/ Simple past	Präteritum	ich *las*, es *regnete*
Personal pronoun	Personalpronomen	*du, er, sie*
Plural	Plural	*Straßen, Menschen*

Englisch	Deutsch	Beispiel
Possessive article	Possessivartikel	*mein* Haus, *deine* Wohnung
Possessive pronoun	Possessiv- pronomen	das ist *meiner*, das sind *unsere*
Prefix	Präfix	*auf*machen, *vor*stellen, *her*stellen
Preposition	Präposition	*auf, zwischen, in, mit*
Present participle	Partizip Präsens (Partizip I)	*schweigend, weinend*
Present perfect	Perfekt	ich *habe gelesen*
Present subjunctive	Konjunktiv I (= Konjunktiv Präsens)	er *sei* müde
Present tense	Präsens	ich *lese*
Pronoun	Pronomen	*du, es, ihm*
Reciprocal pronouns	Reziprok- pronomen	Lisa und Peter lieben *sich/einander*
Reflexive pronoun	Reflexivpronomen	ich wasche *mich*
Relative pronoun	Relativpronomen	das Buch, *das* ich lese
Singular	Singular	*Straße, Mensch*
Subject	Subjekt	*Maria* kauft Schuhe.
Subordinating conjunction	Subjunktion	*dass, als, bevor*
Superlative	Superlativ	das *schönste* Auto, sie fuhren am *schnellsten*
Tense	Tempus	Präsens, Präteritum, Perfekt
Umlaut	Umlaut	*äußerst, möglich, müssen*
Verb	Verb	*lesen, fahren*
Vorgangspassiv	Vorgangspassiv	ich *werde geliebt*
Zustandspassiv	Zustandspassiv	die Arbeit *ist getan*

Lösungen zu den Übungen
Key to the Exercises

Exercise ❶

a) Herr Blum hat eine neue Assistentin. Die Assistentin kommt aus Berlin.
b) Herr Bodet ist Marketingdirektor.
c) Das alte Computerprogramm war langsamer.
d) Frau Radwan fährt heute mit ihrem Kollegen nach Hamburg.
e) Herr Stix ist Österreicher.
f) Der Kopierer ist schon wieder kaputt.
g) Tina macht einen Sprachkurs in Spanien.
h) Während der Besprechung gab es nur Kekse.
i) Die Kolleginnen im Callcenter müssen Geduld aufbringen.
j) Die Sekretärin buchte einen Flug nach Paris.
k) Die Teamassistentin bestellt den Toner und das Papier.
l) Frau Kolar fand im Besprechungszimmer ein Handy.
m) Herr Hundt hat einen neuen Kollegen. Der Kollege kommt aus Leipzig.
n) Frau Danz schreibt einen Bericht. Der Bericht muss morgen fertig sein.
o) Hat die Firma eine Website? Nein, die Firma hat wirklich keine Website.

Exercise ❷

die Freundschaft, das Häuschen, der Zwilling, der Katalysator, die Freiheit, die Erziehung, der Mechanismus, die Schülerin, die Musik, das Brüderlein, die Verspätung, die Station, der Präsident, die Biologie, die Kleinigkeit, der Fabrikant, der König, das Radio, die Verwandtschaft, das Visum, der Winter, der Chef, das Instrument, die Druckerei, die Universität, das Mädchen, das Sortiment

Exercise ❸

a) die Reise   die Reisen
b) das Video   die Videos
c) der Brief   die Briefe
d) die Kassette   die Kassetten
e) das Brötchen   die Brötchen
f) der Tag   die Tage
g) der Bohrer   die Bohrer
h) die Brille   die Brillen
i) das Motorrad   die Motorräder
j) der Stift   die Stifte
k) der Trainee   die Trainees
l) das Jahr   die Jahre
m) die Sekretärin   die Sekretärinnen
n) das Zimmer   die Zimmer
o) der Drucker   die Drucker

Exercise 4

a) Die Verkäuferin half dem Kunden bei der Suche.

b) Das ist mein Kollege Martin.

c) Eine Redewendung besagt: Der Glaube versetzt Berge.

d) Herr Techmer hilft dem Praktikanten bei der Seminararbeit.

e) Die Richterin glaubt dem Zeugen.

f) Die Journalistin interviewt einen Experten.

g) Ich muss mich bei dem Lieferanten beschweren.

h) Der Höhepunkt ist die Ansprache des Bundespräsidenten.

i) Die Fahndung nach dem Terroristen läuft auf Hochtouren.

j) Darüber machten wir uns keine Gedanken.

Exercise 5

a) Mark arbeitet an einer neuen Homepage. Seit er sich mit Webdesign beschäftigt, sieht man ihn nur selten beim Joggen.

b) Julie sucht einen Job als Programmiererin. Sie hat auf diesem Gebiet bereits Erfahrungen gesammelt.

c) Carlos geht ein Jahr nach Deutschland, um seine Sprachkenntnisse zu verbessern. Es wird ihm dort bestimmt gefallen.

d) Hast du daran gedacht, dass Andrea heute eine Stelle als Praktikantin antritt? Du solltest ihr viel Glück wünschen!

e) Herr Smith, ich danke Ihnen, dass Sie gekommen sind.

f) Elena hat noch verschiedene Prüfungen zu absolvieren. Wir werden ihr dabei helfen.

g) Andrew, soll ich dich bei deiner Freundin abholen?

Exercise 6

a) Wer hat diesen Film mit Julia Roberts gesehen?

b) Dieser CD-Player gehört Luca.

c) Wir wussten nicht, wie dieses Diktiergerät funktionierte.

d) Dieses Verhalten gab mir zu denken.

e) Sie sollten diesem Vorfall keine Beachtung schenken.

f) Ich habe dieses Wort noch nie gehört.

g) Diese Fragen wurden mit Hilfe des Internets gelöst.

h) Carla wird diese Wohnung in Hamburg mieten.

Exercise 7

Wir suchen Möbel für unsere Wohnung in Deutschland und finden in einem Einrichtungshaus …

a) … einen Küchentisch. – Dieser ist leider zu groß für unsere Küche.

b) … einen Einbauschrank. – Dieser gefällt uns ausgezeichnet.

c) … eine Eckbank. – Diese ist uns zu teuer.

d) … Stühle für die Essecke. – Diese können wir auf jeden Fall gebrauchen.

e) … einen Schreibtisch. – Dieser ist etwas zu klein.

f) … eine Wohnzimmerlampe. – Diese sollten wir gleich mitnehmen.

Exercise 8

a) Lars kauft sich ein neues Sweatshirt.
b) Ich freue mich über das bestandene Zertifikat.
c) Die Polizei interessierte sich für den Vorfall.
d) Frau Glück und Herr Wein helfen sich.
e) Alexander putzt sich die Zähne.
f) Wir machten uns über den Jahresabschluss Gedanken.
g) Die Kontoauszüge lagen durcheinander auf dem Tisch.
h) Heute gehen wir miteinander ins Kino.

Exercise 9

a) Mit diesem Management wird das Unternehmen nie auf einen grünen Zweig kommen.
   (With the present management this firm is getting nowhere.)
b) Alicée will immer die erste Geige spielen.
   (Alicée never wants to play second fiddle to anyone.)
c) Maria ist gerade noch einmal mit einem blauen Auge davongekommen.
   (Maria has managed to get off lightly again.)
d) Hier geht doch etwas nicht mit rechten Dingen zu.
   (Something definitely seems to be amiss here.)
e) Wir sollten das nicht an die große Glocke hängen.
   (We shouldn't make a big issue of it.)
f) Mike wurde mit offenen Armen empfangen.
   (Mike was welcomed with open arms.)
g) An dieser Aufführung hat der Theaterkritiker kein gutes Haar gelassen.
   (The theatre critic pulled this performance to pieces.)
h) Vor diesem Vorhaben hat er kalte Füße.
   (He's afraid of this job.)
i) Das Ereignis traf uns wie ein Blitz aus heiterem Himmel!
   (The event hit us like a bolt from the blue.)
j) Dies sollte man nicht auf die leichte Schulter nehmen.
   (You shouldn't take something like this lightly.)

Exercise 10

a) groß:
   Eileen ist so groß wie Pia.
   Pia ist größer als Marcus.
   Tom ist von allen Praktikanten am größten.
b) gut:
   Herr Porter spricht so gut Deutsch wie Frau Hundt.
   Frau Hundt spricht besser Deutsch als Sarah.
   Gina spricht am besten Deutsch.
c) gesund:
   Limonade ohne Zucker ist gesund.

Apfelschorle ist allerdings gesünder.
Und ein Glas Wein am Abend ist am gesündesten.
d) viel:
Über naturwissenschaftliche Erscheinungen wusste Inka viel.
Über technische Neuerungen noch mehr.
Und über sprachliche Angelegenheiten am meisten.

Exercise 11

a) Das habe ich mir eben vorgenommen.
b) Daran hat Vivian in der Eile halt nicht mehr gedacht.
c) Wo habe ich bloß meine Uhr hingelegt?
d) Was ist denn hier los?
e) Das ist aber großzügig von Ihnen!
f) Genau das habe ich doch gerade befürchtet!
g) Andy hat das wohl nicht so ernst genommen.
h) Dies konnte ich mir ja denken!

Exercise 12

a) Am Montag hat Hardy eine Agenda für das nächste Meeting erhalten.
b) Von ihrem Mann hat Rebecca dieses Geschenk bekommen.
c) Um 10:30 Uhr nehmen die Touristen an einer Stadtführung teil.
d) Heute hat Yvonne einen Termin in der Autowerkstatt.
e) Den Gesprächstermin hätte Frau Simon wahrnehmen sollen.
f) Mit dem Bus fährt Margarita in die Stadt.

Exercise 13

a) Gehe ich heute Abend mit Muriel in die Stadt?
b) Besuchen wir am Wochenende meine Cousine?
c) Muss ich mich am Samstag auf das Bewerbungsgespräch vorbereiten?
d) Treffen wir uns heute Nachmittag auf einen Kaffee?
e) Beschäftige ich mich gerade mit den Regeln der deutschen Grammatik?
f) Hat das Training bereits begonnen?

Exercise 14

a) Kann Andrew Deutsch sprechen? – Ja, er möchte aber seine Kenntnisse noch erweitern.
b) Musst du heute noch lernen? – Ja, ich muss!
c) Ich darf Ihnen doch bestimmt eine kleine Erfrischung anbieten, oder …? – Ja, Sie dürfen.
d) Bitte beachten Sie, dass Sie auf Bahnhöfen nicht rauchen dürfen.
e) An dieser Stelle dürfen Sie nicht parken.
f) Du möchtest mit mir noch einige Worte sprechen?
g) Über das Jobsharing müssen wir uns nochmals Gedanken machen.
h) Hier sollten Sie leise sein.

Exercise 15

a) verfallen: Durch die Euro-Einführung verfallen bestimmte Briefmarken.
b) anfangen: Der Film „Harry Potter" fängt um 20:00 Uhr an.
c) übersetzen: Herr Brown übersetzt den Text ins Deutsche.
d) umschreiben: Der Lehrer umschreibt die unbekannte Vokabel mit Synonymen.
e) abgeben: Der Kurier gibt das Paket an der Pforte ab.
f) umziehen: Am Sonntag zieht Pamela in die neue Wohnung um.
g) gefallen: Der Dom und die Steinerne Brücke in Regensburg gefallen mir.
h) ausfallen: Das Training-on-the-Job fällt heute aus.
i) unterstellen: Dieses böswillige Verhalten unterstellte man Kim.
j) zerfallen: Die Tagesordnung zerfällt in acht umfangreiche Punkte.

Exercise 16

a) Bewerben Sie sich bitte um den Job als Trainee!
b) Nimm bitte an dem Kurs in der Sprachenschule teil!
c) Rauchen Sie bitte nicht im Gang!
d) Frag bitte, wenn dir eine Redewendung nicht bekannt ist!
e) Kommt bitte pünktlich!

Exercise 17

a) Herr White buchte für Donnerstag einen Flug nach Deutschland.
Herr White hat für Donnerstag einen Flug nach Deutschland gebucht.
b) Er kam am Flughafen Berlin-Tegel an und stieg in das nächste Taxi.
Er ist am Flughafen Berlin-Tegel angekommen und [ist] in das nächste Taxi gestiegen.
c) Dieses fuhr Herrn White in das Hotel „Zum Goldenen Stern".
Dieses hat Herrn White in das Hotel „Zum Goldenen Stern" gefahren.
d) An der Rezeption erhielt er die Schlüssel für sein Zimmer.
An der Rezeption hat er die Schlüssel für sein Zimmer erhalten.
e) Um 15:00 Uhr traf sich Herr White mit seinen Geschäftspartnern.
Um 15:00 Uhr hat sich Herr White mit seinen Geschäftspartnern getroffen.
f) Diese erklärten ihm die neue geschäftliche Situation und baten um Verständnis.
Diese haben ihm die neue geschäftliche Situation erklärt und [haben] um Verständnis gebeten.
g) Herr White unterbrach die Verhandlungen und zog einen neuen Termin in Betracht.
Herr White hat die Verhandlungen unterbrochen und [hat] einen neuen Termin in Betracht gezogen.
h) Am nächsten Morgen holte Herr White seine Frau vom Flughafen ab.
Am nächsten Morgen hat Herr White seine Frau vom Flughafen abgeholt.

i)   Gemeinsam verbrachten sie einige Tage in Berlin.
     Gemeinsam haben sie einige Tage in Berlin verbracht.
j)   Frau und Herr White sahen sich noch am selben Tag das Brandenburger
     Tor an.
     Frau und Herr White haben sich noch am selben Tag das Brandenburger
     Tor angesehen.
k)   Am folgenden Tag besichtigten sie den Reichstag.
     Am folgenden Tag haben sie den Reichstag besichtigt.
l)   Am letzten Tag ihres Urlaubs fuhren sie auf den Fernsehturm und
     warfen einen Blick auf die Dächer Berlins.
     Am letzten Tag ihres Urlaubs sind sie auf den Fernsehturm gefahren
     und haben einen Blick auf die Dächer Berlins geworfen.

Exercise 18

a)   Nachdem wir einen Nachsendeauftrag bei der Post gestellt hatten,
     fuhren wir in den Urlaub.
b)   Nachdem Eileen die Führerscheinprüfung bestanden hatte, feierten
     wir das erfreuliche Ereignis mit einem Gläschen Sekt.
c)   Nachdem Marcus die Vor- und Nachteile dargestellt hatte, gingen wir
     zur Aussprache über.
d)   Nachdem der Chef von seiner Auslandsreise zurückgekommen war,
     wurde das umstrittene Projekt nochmals besprochen.
e)   Nachdem die Abteilungsleiter eingetroffen waren, diskutierten wir
     über das weitere Vorgehen.

Exercise 19

a)   Herr White wird für Donnerstag einen Flug nach Deutschland buchen.
b)   Er wird am Flughafen Berlin-Tegel ankommen und [wird] in das nächste
     Taxi steigen.
c)   Dieses wird Herrn White in das Hotel „Zum Goldenen Stern" fahren.
d)   An der Rezeption wird er die Schlüssel für sein Zimmer erhalten.
e)   Um 15:00 Uhr wird sich Herr White mit seinen Geschäftspartnern
     treffen.
f)   Diese werden ihm die neue geschäftliche Situation erklären und
     [werden] um Verständnis bitten.
g)   Herr White wird seine Verhandlungen unterbrechen und [wird] einen
     neuen Termin in Betracht ziehen.
h)   Am nächsten Morgen wird Herr White seine Frau vom Flughafen
     abholen.
i)   Gemeinsam werden sie einige Tage in Berlin verbringen.
j)   Frau und Herr White werden sich noch am selben Tag das Brandenburger
     Tor ansehen.
k)   Am folgenden Tag werden sie den Reichstag besichtigen.
l)   Am letzten Tag ihres Urlaubs werden sie auf den Fernsehturm fahren
     und [werden] einen Blick auf die Dächer Berlins werfen.

Exercise 20

a) Herr Miller sagt, er sei mit seiner neuen Marketingassistentin sehr zufrieden.
   (oder:) Herr Miller sagt, dass er mit seiner neuen Marketingassistentin sehr zufrieden sei.
b) Frau Dinz erläutert, durch das neue Computerprogramm könnten wir die Absatzzahlen schneller ermitteln.
   (oder:) Frau Dinz erläutert, dass wir durch das neue Computerprogramm die Absatzzahlen schneller ermitteln könnten.
c) Der Verkäufer erklärt, das neue Handy verfüge über eine USB-Schnittstelle.
   (oder:) Der Verkäufer erklärt, dass das neue Handy über eine USB-Schnittstelle verfüge.
d) Die Angestellte erwidert, durch mehr Personal erreichten wir eine bessere Kundenbindung (oder: … würden wir eine bessere Kundenbindung erreichen).
   (oder:) Die Angestellte erwidert, dass wir durch mehr Personal eine bessere Kundenbindung erreichten (oder: … erreichen würden).
e) Der Chef sagt, er sei mit der Arbeitsweise von Frau Gordon sehr zufrieden.
   (oder:) Der Chef sagt, dass er mit der Arbeitsweise von Frau Gordon sehr zufrieden sei.

Exercise 21

a) Dürfte ich Sie kurz stören?
b) Könntest du das für mich kopieren?
c) Das wäre wirklich nett von dir.
d) Wenn ich eine eigene Firma hätte, dann würde ich mit den Mitarbeitern jeden Morgen Tai-Chi machen.
e) So eine Katastrophe! Das alles wäre nicht passiert, wenn ich besser aufgepasst hätte!

Exercise 22

a) Im 15. Jahrhundert wurden die ersten Bücher in Europa gedruckt.
b) Johann Wolfgang von Goethe wurde in Frankfurt geboren.
c) 1895 wurden die Röntgenstrahlen entdeckt.
d) 1957 wurde die Europäische Wirtschaftsgemeinschaft gegründet.
e) In den 60er Jahren wurden in Deutschland viele Universitäten gebaut.
f) 2002 wurde der Euro eingeführt.

Exercise 23

a) Die Abschlussfeier fand bei meinem Bruder Patrick statt.

b) Der Autofahrer ist gegen den Baum gefahren.

c) Die Auszubildenden stehen im Kreis um ihren Trainer.

d) Aufgrund der Globalisierung werden Sprachkenntnisse immer wichtiger.

e) Die Touristen-Information befindet sich gegenüber dem Rathaus.

f) Trotz der zahlreichen Regeln beherrscht Axel die deutsche Grammatik gut.

g) Seit einem Jahr hat Steve einen Job als Webdesigner.

h) Während der Sommermonate befinden sich im Bistro um die Ecke nur wenige Gäste.

i) Ramona ist am Wochenende zu ihrer Schwester gefahren.

j) Der Bankangestellte holt das Geld aus dem Tresor.

k) Maggie und Geneviève haben für den weltweiten Frieden protestiert.

l) Der Schlüssel war zwischen dem Gepäck.

Exercise 24

a) Mike ist enttäuscht, weil die Vergütung nicht seinen Vorstellungen entspricht.

b) Peer wirkt gelassen, seit er täglich Yoga-Übungen macht.

c) Lucia spielt seit drei Jahren Gitarre und [sie] surft auch gerne im Internet.

d) Victor freut sich, dass er nächste Woche in den Urlaub gehen kann.

e) Das Seminar fand nicht statt, da es zu wenig Teilnehmer gab.

f) Frau Wilice besucht das Deutsche Museum oder [sie] geht auf den Marienplatz.

Exercise 25

a) der Gummibaum

b) der Ringordner

c) das Druckerpapier

d) der Lichtschalter

e) der Schnellläufer

f) der Wohnungsmarkt

g) die Überbevölkerung

h) die Handytasche

i) der Nassschnee

j) das Hellblau

k) der Vorabend

Exercise 26

a) Simons Katze ist entlaufen.

b) Herr Franklin muss noch aus-/einchecken.

c) Marilyn ist krank und sollte sich daher zudecken.

d) Die Reisefreiheit war als wichtiger Fortschritt zu betrachten.

e) Das Bungee-Jumping sieht gefährlich aus.

f) Frau Setlur macht einen jugendlichen Eindruck.

g) Wir müssen das Geschenk einpacken.

h) Sollen wir Sie das Stück mitnehmen?

i) Auf dieses Angebot werden Sie bestimmt noch zurückkommen.

j) Die Freundschaft mit Jenny war mir viel wert.

k) Die Assistentin stellte das Projekt fertig.

l) Wir hoffen, dass Sie jetzt nicht mehr sprachlos sind!

Deutsches Register German Index

Englisches Register English Index

 A

accusative 29 f.
adjectival ending 52
adjective 51
adverb 60
alternatives for the passive 128
article 12
auxiliary verb 75

 C

capital letter 21
case 29 ff.
cause 61
comparative 56
comparison 56
composing new words 158
coordinating conjunctions 140

D

dative 29 f.
declension 32
definite article 13 ff.
demonstrative pronoun 42
deriving new words 162
direct speech 113 f.

F

feminine 12, 24
formal imperative 93
future 125
future perfect 126
future tense 109

G

gender 12, 21
genitive 29 f.

I

imperative 68, 92 ff.
indefinite article 13
indirect speech 113 f.
infinitive 25, 75
infinitive clause 151
informal imperative 92

interrogative pronoun 46 f.
irregular verb 96, 165 ff.

 M

manner 61
masculine 12, 22
mixed verb 98, 165 ff.
modal particle 64
modal verb 77, 98, 127

N

n-declension 33
neuter 12, 23
nominative 29 f.
noun 21
number 12

O

occupations 18

 P

passive 121
passive describing a state 129
passive expressing action 122
past participle 99
past perfect 99, 104, 125
past perfect subjunctive 127
past simple 96, 124
past subjunctive 117, 126
personal pronoun 37
plural 12, 26
positive 56
possessive article 40, 149
possessive pronoun 40
prefix 82
preposition 16, 132
prepositions that vary 135
present perfect 99
present subjunctive 113, 126
present tense 89, 123
pronoun 36
proper names 18

Alles rund ums Verb – zum Nachschlagen und Üben!

- 70 Konjugationstabellen mit Anwendungsbeispielen

- Tipps & Tricks zum effektiven Lernen

- Pro Verb eine Doppelseite mit allen wichtigen Informationen

- Extra-Kapitel Grammatik rund ums Verb

- Inklusive Konjugationstrainer mit abwechslungsreichen Übungsformen